# THE
# PROMISE *of* ENOUGH

SEVEN PRINCIPLES OF TRUE ABUNDANCE

# T H E
# PROMISE *of* ENOUGH

## SEVEN PRINCIPLES OF TRUE ABUNDANCE

# EMILY FREEMAN

### WITH PAINTINGS BY SIMON DEWEY

DESERET
BOOK

Salt Lake City, Utah

*For McKinley, an insight extraordinaire,*
*And JJ, an enthusiasm aficionado,*
*Who have taught me to embrace every last bit of*
*knowledge and joy life has to offer.*
*No one could ask for a better cheering section.*

Visit us at DeseretBook.com

For more information about Simon Dewey's artwork, visit www.altusfineart.com

Library of Congress Cataloging-in-Publication Data

Freeman, Emily, 1969-
    The promise of enough : seven principles of true abundance / Emily Freeman ; illustrated by Simon Dewey.
       p. cm.
    Includes bibliographical references and index.
    ISBN 978-1-60641-143-8 (hardbound : alk. paper)
    1. Christian life—Mormon authors.    I. Dewey, Simon.    II. Title.
    BX8656.F78 2009
    248.4—dc22                                                                    2009017923

Printed in the United States of America
Inland Graphics, Menomonee Falls, WI

10  9  8  7  6  5  4  3  2  1

I AM COME THAT THEY MIGHT

HAVE LIFE, AND THAT THEY MIGHT HAVE

IT MORE ABUNDANTLY.

—John 10:10

# CONTENTS

# An Invitation from the Author

*This book is meant to be written in.*

I have found that my favorite books are those that I have left a mark in. Sometimes the words are simply underlined. Other times I will place a star in the margin next to a certain line or paragraph. But, if you look carefully through my library, you will find that my favorite passages are those marked with a star and an exclamation point in the margin. It is my way of reminding myself, "This is important; someday you might want to think about this again."

Sometimes I leave myself a handwritten note somewhere in the blank spaces on the page . . . a reminder of something I've learned or want to remember. Then, when I have finished the book, it's like I have left a part of me there. It fascinates me to return to those pages years later to see where I have come from and what I have learned. Over time the books that I have marked have become a part of me; somehow marking the page has left a marking on my heart. You will find several journal pages at the end of this book. I hope you will fill them with your thoughts and your testimony.

So, before you begin this book, may I kindly suggest that you find something to write with. Then settle into a quiet haven that allows plenty of room for thought.

Experience has taught me that somewhere between doodling and brainstorming personal discoveries are made.

True discovery begins with introspection.

Introspection requires pondering.

Pondering leads to understanding.

What we understand, we hope to remember.

To be remembered, it must be written . . .

Abundance.
It is what He knows best.
The principle of promise.
The underlying theme of His life.

It is the tender behind the mercy.
The unconditional behind the love.
The height, breadth, and depth behind
    the understanding.

It has never been otherwise and remains
    true today.

And so,
when weary souls long for the abundant life,
it is to One source they must turn.

For He is known now just as He was known
    in times of old.

He is
The Giver
of every good gift.

# Introduction

They had come for different reasons.

Some sought healing and, filled with anticipation, they came. Now, cautiously hoping, they watched the humble man moving through the crowd. With faith stirring in their souls, they waited for the opportunity to petition at the feet of Him who offered miracles.

Some came with a desire to know something of this man who taught in parables, who spoke of their traditions in unexpected ways. They came longing to hear more, to gain an understanding from Him who offered answers.

And then there were those who were aching with a sorrow that was fresh and deep. They had lost their shepherd, and now searched for another to lead them. Here was the one who John had baptized. And so with trepidation they came, clinging to shattered memories, to learn at the feet of Him who offered comfort.

Hours passed, and still they remained. Even as the sun began to set they were drawn to Him, drawn to what He offered, drawn to the Giver.

He had known they would come, just as *He knew what He was about to do.* The Giver had walked among them with patience and compassion, to teach them many things (Mark 6:34), and to heal those in need of healing (Luke 9:11). Finally, when the day was far spent, He turned to His disciples asking, "Whence shall we buy bread, that these may eat?" (John 6:5).

The unexpected question came as a surprise. The small group traveled with little provisions and money was scarce. Even if they were to offer everything they had, it would not be enough. The obvious solution was to dismiss the multitude and allow them to return to the village to find food and shelter. But this was not what He had asked of them. And so they gathered to converse. *What did they have to offer?* What He asked would require sacrifice. They would have to give of their own.

One of the disciples turned to the young lad. The boy had followed behind them all day, carrying a small basket containing what was to have been their supper. They were not accustomed to fine meals, and had learned to get by with the very humblest of provisions. This day, what little money they carried with them was used to purchase the poorest of breads—five barley loaves. There had been enough left over to purchase two small, salted fish, commonly sold along the shores of Galilee. It was hardly enough for them, and the disciple could not help but ask, *What are they among so many?*

Carefully the lad made his way through the crowd to the place where the Giver sat. He placed the basket at His feet, and knelt. The lad was in awe of these men he traveled with, for no matter what the Giver asked, *His disciples did not hesitate to obey.* Even now, he watched as the disciples gathered the people into groups to prepare for the meal. Somehow these men had set aside their doubt, but he still could not help but wonder from whence the meal would come. Finally the disciples returned. The lad looked out across the great company of men, women, and children who sat scattered across the green grass. There were well over 5,000 people patiently watching the Giver who had laid out the meager provisions of bread and fish at His feet.

The lad watched in amazement as the Giver took the bread and *gave thanks.* Such gratitude for this simplest of foods surprised the boy. And then, breaking it into pieces, He began to hand the bread to His disciples and they, in turn, gave to the multitude, one by one, until each had received. The people ate until they were filled, *as much as they would,* even the small lad.

And when the meal was finished, the Giver asked His disciples to *gather what remained.* Even now, the miracle of it all—the gift—was beyond understanding.

Twelve disciples.
Twelve wicker baskets, filled to overflowing.
Enough, and some to spare.
*Abundance.*

# Finding the Wellspring

*"I will pour out my Spirit upon you, and great shall be your blessing—
yea, even more than if you should obtain treasures of earth."*

—D&C 19:38

It was one of those times in life when I believed wholeheartedly in the old adage, "Bad things always happen in threes." I was flat in bed with a complicated pregnancy; my husband, Greg, was seriously considering a job change that would negatively influence our already tight cash flow; and to top it all off, my son, Josh, who was supposed to get the cast taken off his broken arm that day, had just taken a hard fall, breaking the joint in his thumb. Greg came home from work to take Josh to the hospital to get the first cast removed, and returned hours later with Josh's arm again set in a cast for another four weeks.

That evening, our bishop and his wife stopped by unannounced for a quick visit. The house was a wreck, Greg and I were discussing our financial situation, and I had spent the majority of the evening in tears because I had been unable to accompany Josh to the hospital and I was tired of being in bed.

Needless to say, our home was not a happy place.

The bishop walked into our living room and glanced at a small, hand-painted piece of wood that was sitting on the table. The wooden block had one simple word painted on its surface. The bishop put his hand on his wife's shoulder and pointed to the piece of wood. "Look, Terri," he said, "the Freemans have *abundance*."

We laughed and I set the record straight. We didn't have abundance . . . abundance was what we were hoping for. In fact, the only thing we had an abundance of right then was adversity.

The next morning, and for many mornings after, I looked at that wooden block and wondered when the abundance would come. After some time, the word itself began to intrigue me and I found myself pondering what having abundance really meant. I turned to the scripture in John 10:10 that reads, "I am come that they might have life, and that they might have it more abundantly." I had always thought abundance had to do with wealth or prosperity, but this scripture made me wonder if perhaps I was wrong. I was intrigued with the thought that abundance had to do with *life*. Was living an abundant life different from the way I was currently living? My pondering led me to realize that although I was desperately seeking abundance, perhaps I wasn't exactly sure what I was looking for, or where I should look to find it.

The dictionary explained abundance as an overflowing fullness: enough and to spare. I was immediately reminded of a wellspring. When I was very young, my family would visit Cascade Springs, located at the top of American Fork Canyon. I remember how my uncle helped us find the source of the spring water. We walked along small rivers and past waterfalls until we reached the higher ground where we found the wellspring, a place where the water flowed out of seemingly impermeable rock before it began cascading down the mountain. The water never stopped flowing; there was an overflowing fullness. In fact, each day seven million gallons of water comes through that rock base to feed the springs. Cascade Springs is a wellspring of abundance. This reminder reinforced my desire to find the wellspring I was searching for.

We live in a time when people are emphasizing the need to simplify, cut back, and do without. Because this message surrounds us on every side, it can be hard to imagine a life filled with abundance. The world would have us believe that abundance is a fancy house, or a new car, or a ski boat, or a cabin. The scriptures give us a different perspective. The Savior taught, "A man's life consisteth not in the abundance of the things which he possesseth" (Luke 12:15). I have come to believe that to be true. Abundance is not defined by what we own. Instead, abundance is a way of life. It comes as we begin to discover the promise of enough and the miracle of "some to spare" within the everyday moments of our life.

I wanted to learn to live abundantly. My search led me to become more aware of the people I knew who already lived an abundant life. I also discovered that there are many scriptural examples of people who have learned the secret for living the abundant life. One of my favorite examples is found in the story of Nephi.

The beginning of the Book of Mormon talks of great changes for Nephi and his family as they leave Jerusalem and wander into the wilderness. This part of the story contains experiences that are discouraging and filled with affliction. Nephi's family left behind their home full of luxuries and possessions. They also left behind their friends. On the surface it is easy to assume that they had walked away from great abundance and into great poverty. But was that really the case?

As this wilderness experience is described by Nephi and then later by his brothers Laman and Lemuel, it is interesting to read the differences in attitude. Nephi tells us, "And we did travel and wade through much affliction in the wilderness. . . . And *so great were the blessings of the Lord upon us*" (1 Nephi 17:1–2; emphasis added).

On the other hand, Laman and Lemuel said, "Behold, these many years we have suffered in the wilderness, which time we might have enjoyed our possessions and the land of our inheritance; yea, *and we might have been happy*" (1 Nephi 17:21; emphasis added).

Interestingly, they were both talking about the very same experience. The difference was in how they viewed that experience. Because he had found the wellspring for living the abundant life, Nephi's eyes were opened to see great blessings, no matter the situation. Laman and Lemuel, though, only saw suffering. For one brother, recognizing the blessings led to a life filled with abundance, but for the others, a life of unhappiness. There is a lesson to be learned from this story. I don't want to look back at my life and think I *might* have been happy. I want to learn to recognize the blessings at every juncture. I want to find the secret for living the abundant life.

Stop for a moment and think about your own life. This will require examining your heart. Do you feel that something is lacking? If you were to try to fill that place with an abundance of something, what would it be? Perhaps you are lonely, and you long for an abundance of love. Maybe you suffer from an illness, and you long for an abundance of health. Some may long for peace or comfort. Others may long for more time or an abundance of joy. Each of us, for one reason or another, longs for abundance. I believe that it is the yearning that inspires the search. Without that yearning, there would be no motivation for the journey.

This longing for abundance reminds me of the story found in John 6:5–13, the miracle of the loaves and the fishes. On the afternoon of the miracle, the disciples went through a learning process that led them to find the wellspring of abundance. We too can learn a powerful lesson on abundance as we ponder the message found in that scriptural event. A careful look into this story will help us discover seven key principles that will lead us to discover the wellspring of abundance in our own life. These principles include the importance of understanding God's will, recognizing your own potential, giving all you have, letting obedience lead to belief, remembering gratitude, learning to be content, and trusting that Christ's love passeth all understanding.

The beginning of each chapter in this book will explain a principle of abundance as found in the miracle of the loaves and the fishes. The rest of the chapter will include life lessons and stories that emphasize the importance of that principle.

At the end of each chapter are one or two questions that will allow you to ponder how living each principle will lead you to a life filled with abundance.

When you come to these questions, I hope you will take to heart a few words of encouragement from President Thomas S. Monson, "Make the most of today."[1] I would suggest you take a minute to stop and consider your own life. Perhaps you could take an entire day to reflect on what those questions mean to you. Maybe you will feel inclined to write some of your thoughts along the margins, or in a personal journal. When you are making the most of every day, you can't help but discover abundance.

Looking back, I realize that in my search to discover the wellspring of abundance the answers did not come all at once. Instead, knowledge has come incrementally. As I am ready, the next piece is given. It seems that once I have learned the value of one lesson, another is waiting right behind. And so that is the way this book has been written—one thought at a time, with another lesson waiting right behind. This will allow you to move at your own pace, giving you time to discover, introspect, ponder, understand, remember, and if you choose, to write down what you have learned. My hope is to share the principles, stories, scriptures, and nuggets of knowledge that have influenced my search. In keeping with the theme of the book, I have hopefully included enough, and probably some to spare.

Is abundance something you long for?

Have you ever found yourself gathering what constitutes a small and simple offering, kneeling at the feet of the Lord, and pleading with Him to make it more?

If so, then consider yourself a fellow seeker—a welcome traveler on this journey to discover the promise of enough, and the miracle of some to spare.

May your search for abundance allow you to discover blessings unmeasured, but more importantly, may you be led to find the wellspring from whence those blessings flow.

He had known they would come, just as
He knew what He was about to do.

# The First Principle

## UNDERSTAND GOD'S WILL

*"The Lord is good to all: and his tender mercies are over all his works."*

—Psalm 145:9

It was not happenstance that led to the miracle of the loaves and the fishes. In fact, as we look carefully through the stories of the life of Christ we see many examples where Christ took a certain route, visited a certain home, or stopped in a certain location for a specific purpose. He knew before He arrived that a life-changing experience, whether in the form of a teaching moment or a miracle, was about to take place. We see this clearly in the story of the loaves and the fishes when John tells us that, long before the miracle occurred, the Savior "knew what he would do" (John 6:6). The same is true in each of our lives; whether we are facing feast or famine, the Lord is aware of us, He has miracles in store for us, and He knows what He is about to do.

It had been described as an easy hike up a barely flowing riverbed. Flat *almost* the whole way, with a *few* slippery places. The purpose of the hike was to reach a breathtaking arch at the end. Now, I am not a hiker, but hiking up a riverbed with

13

four to six inches of water flowing over my bare feet intrigued me, and so I found myself in a group of twenty-four people, preparing to begin the adventure.

Because only one person in the group had been on the hike before, he became the leader. We trusted his advice and we followed him. As the group spread out, we watched for his footprints in the sand along the edges of the riverbank leading the way. The first challenge came when we reached the waterfall. Our leader was waiting for us there to make sure we were prepared to climb up the rock wall next to the waterfall. He had helpers with him, some to support us and some to lift us over the obstacle. He was waiting again to warn us as we reached the part of the hike where the rocky river bottom was covered with lichen, making it so slippery that each step had to be taken with care. Every time we needed direction or counsel, our leader was there to guide us through.

At the end of two and a half hours we arrived at the base of a huge, sand-covered hill. We were exhausted and sore. It seemed we would never reach the arch, and the mountain of sand was almost more than we could surmount. Pausing for breath at the bottom, we were encouraged by those hikers who were at the top and had finished the journey—the view made it all worthwhile, they promised. The hill was so steep that the arch remained hidden from view until we reached the very tip, and then, suddenly, there it was. Rising a hundred feet into the sky, framing the river that ran through the narrow canyon. Magnificent. Remarkable. I stood in wonder and admired the greatness of God, grateful that I had been willing to trust our leader, who had encouraged us to embark on the adventure because he knew the reward that awaited us at the end.

In the book of Joshua, we read of a group of people who also found themselves on an adventure, hiking through a riverbed. In a scene reminiscent of crossing the Red Sea, Joshua prepares the people of Israel to cross the Jordan River. I love the lessons we are taught from this story. First, Joshua tells the people of Israel that they must watch the leaders who were carrying the ark of the covenant "that ye may know the way by which ye must go: *for ye have not passed this way heretofore*" (Joshua 3:4; emphasis added). Then, he asks the people to prepare themselves, encouraging them, "for to morrow the Lord will do wonders among you" (Joshua 3:5). And the Lord indeed promises Joshua, "I will be with thee" (Joshua 3:7). As the people began their adventure, they did as Joshua had asked—they watched their leaders. As soon as the soles of the priests rested in the waters of the Jordan River, the waters "stood in a heap," and the people passed through the riverbed. Miraculously, the priests "stood firm on dry ground in the midst" (Joshua 3:17), until all of the people had passed through safely and witnessed the greatness of God.

When I come to a life adventure that is unfamiliar to me, I think of these lessons in Joshua and say to myself, *"I have not passed this way heretofore."* I am reminded of the importance of following my leaders, and trust in my belief in a God who will do wonders in my life. There is a sweet assurance that comes from knowing that He will be with me throughout the adventure to warn me of dangers ahead, and to lift and encourage me along the way. My trust in His will is strengthened each time I acknowledge His wonders in my life and in the moments when I experience His greatness.

Sometimes life will lead us to wonder if God is aware of our circumstances. When burdens overtake us, whether they are financial, emotional, physical, or spiritual, we must remember that He is aware of us and that He has a plan for us. Our complete trust in the Lord will allow Him to work wonders in our life so that we can begin to experience abundance.

Thus, the first principle of abundance comes from learning to trust God's will and then allowing Him to work wonders in our life. Through our willingness to live this principle, God's greatness will be made manifest and we will be led to discover His abundance. "I would that ye should remember, and always retain in remembrance, the greatness of God, . . . and his goodness and long-suffering towards you" (Mosiah 4:11).

I will be honest, Job scares me. I should probably clarify that I am not necessarily scared of Job, the man; I am scared of Job, the story. Reading his story brings out too much of the realist in me and reminds me how fragile life can be. But experience has taught me that great wisdom can be found in each of the stories that have been included in the scriptures.

Job was a just and perfect man who had been blessed abundantly because of his righteousness, his charity, and his good deeds. God was well pleased with His servant, but Satan questioned, "Doth Job fear God for nought?" (Job 1:9), asking God if Job was righteous only because his life was so easy. But the Lord did not doubt Job. He told Satan, "Behold, all that he hath is in thy power; only upon himself put not forth thine hand" (Job 1:12).

Imagine Job's surprise as his life unexpectedly began to crumble. His property was destroyed, his children were killed, and he became very ill. And yet, in the midst of his afflictions, he turned to the Lord in prayer and testified of God's greatness, and his own confidence in the Lord saying, "Though he slay me, yet will I trust in him" (Job 13:15).

The wisdom I like best from Job's story is found in the last few chapters because this is where we begin to understand what Job means by the greatness of God. How important is this understanding? For me it is the key to the entire story. First, Job describes the greatness of God by saying, "God is great . . . for he maketh small the drops of water . . . which the clouds do drop and distil upon man abundantly" (Job 36:26–28). What a beautiful image. Have you ever been outside in a rainstorm? When I was young my favorite time to pick raspberries in my backyard was during a rainstorm. There was a good reason for this . . . I hate bees. My mom suggested picking raspberries with the sprinklers on, but it didn't work as well. The small drops of water from the sprinklers did not reach all the way through the raspberry bushes, and the bees learned to move to the areas where the water couldn't reach. But when the rain fell, the small drops of water fell equally on all of the raspberry bushes, and all of the bees left. I could pick the raspberries without any fear of being stung. I think of that experience when I read this scripture in Job. I imagine God showering down blessings upon each one of us, chasing our fears away, sending abundance.

Job goes on to explain that God's greatness includes His ability to give in abundance (Job 36:31). Although this seems to contradict what we know of Job's story as so much was taken from him, the principle is clearly shown as we discover the great blessing that comes at the end of Job's life. After having lost everything, including his health, his prosperity, his friends, and his family, the scriptures tell us that "the Lord gave Job twice as much as he had before" (Job 42:10). In fact, "the Lord blessed the latter end of Job more than his beginning" (Job 42:12), until he had received a fullness, enough and some to spare, until he had been blessed abundantly.

*I imagine God showering down blessings upon each one of us, chasing our fears away, sending abundance.*

Have you ever had a Job-like experience? One where you faced a seemingly insurmountable trial regarding finances, health, or relationships? Those are my least favorite moments. They leave me feeling worried and frantic at the end of the day. And sometimes those days turn into anxious, stress-filled weeks—or even months. During those times, I have learned that there is only one remedy. Like Job, I try to remember the greatness of God. Trusting in God's matchless power has led me to believe that He is greater than any problem I will encounter during my mortal existence. Often it is only after I have taken the time to remember God's greatness and His ability to work wonders in my life that I finally find the peace I am looking for. Then, I set a plan to do my very best to solve the problem, knowing that after all I can do, He will take care of the rest. I know why Job remembered and testified of the greatness of God in the midst of his adversity—without that belief, there would have been no reason to endure.

God knew all along what would happen to Job. He knew about the trials, but He also knew about the blessings. And, more importantly, He knew about the learning, and what it would take to make Job's life-experience complete. Although his life was filled with disappointment and discouragement, Job was blessed abundantly. Elder Joseph B. Wirthlin explains, "The Lord compensates the faithful for every loss. That which is taken away from those who love the Lord will be added unto them in His own way. While it may not come at the time we desire, the faithful will know that every tear today will eventually be returned a hundredfold with tears of rejoicing and gratitude."[2]

God is great. He is greater than any problem, discouragement, or adversity we will face. We can learn an important lesson from the story of Job: even in the midst of trial and disappointment, great blessings of abundance are in store. We must learn to trust God's will for us, but more importantly, we must learn to trust that His will for us is good, and that the promised abundance will eventually come.

"Great is his wisdom, marvelous are his ways, and the extent of his doings none can find out. . . . And to them will I reveal all mysteries, yea, . . . will I make known unto them the *good pleasure of my will* concerning all things. . . .

"For by my Spirit will I enlighten them, and by my power will I make known unto them the secrets of my will—yea, even those things which eye has not seen, nor ear heard, nor yet entered into the heart of man" (D&C 76:2, 7, 10).

❦

I will never forget one of the darkest times of my life. For three years I had struggled with several overwhelming burdens that had exhausted me emotionally, spiritually, and physically. The burdens had come one right after the other, with almost no pause in-between. I developed severe migraines from the stress. The headaches would come late in the afternoons, sometimes three or four times a week, and would not leave before I had spent most of the evening throwing up. I also found myself slipping into depression. As the depression deepened, I remember Greg asking me, "When are you ever going to come back?" and my fearful answer, "I might not."

One particular day I remember desperately trying to find help. For almost a year I had tried to lean on my husband, my close friends, and my family to find the strength I needed, but it was not enough. No one seemed to know how to pull me out of the despair that surrounded me. With nowhere left to turn, I pulled my health insurance card out of my wallet and flipped it over where there was a list of phone numbers, including one that said, "If you are in need of mental health assistance, call this number." So I called the number. A woman answered and I began to explain my situation in great detail. Obviously it was a poor attempt at an explanation, because as soon as I finished, the woman replied, "Oh, honey, you just need a massage."

Although it is funny now, at the time I was devastated. That phone number had been my last resort. I remember going to bed that night and waiting until Greg and all of the kids were asleep, and then I cried. I mentally reviewed a list of everyone I knew, thinking there must be someone who would know how to help me heal. But at the end of two hours none of the names seemed right. There was absolutely no one I could think of who could understand where I was and how to help me out of that dark place. I resigned myself to the fact that I was really on my own, and then I heard a small voice whisper to my heart, "Heavenly Father knows."

A sense of calm came over me as I realized the words were true. Heavenly Father did know. He knew what had happened, He knew the heavy burden I carried, and because of that, He would know how to help me through. I began to pray. It is a prayer I will never forget as long as I live. I was led to lean on the Savior. In Him I found a reservoir of peace, comfort, and strength beyond my own. I found a place to heal. I firmly believe that the only way I made it through those dark days was knowing that the night would come, and with it, the opportunity for another heartfelt conversation with God and the promise of peace. I took great comfort in the knowledge that Heavenly Father was aware of my situation, and that He would see me through. Lehi said, "O how great the holiness of our God! For he knoweth all things, and there is not anything save he knows it" (2 Nephi 9:20).

We can find comfort in this important truth—God knows. We are encouraged to "Trust in the Lord with all thine heart; and lean not unto thine own understanding. In all thy ways acknowledge him, and he shall direct thy paths" (Proverbs 3:5–6). God knows the end from the beginning. He knows what we have been through, and He knows where we are going. He knows how to protect us from the dangers that surround us, and He knows how to succor us during the trials that would otherwise destroy us.

Abundant moments will begin to fill our life as we learn to trust completely in God's will for us. And the more we come to believe that His will for us is good, the easier it will become to trust Him completely. We must believe that He will prepare a way for us to accomplish what He has in mind for us, even when we feel consumed by a trial that seems to overpower us. There is great comfort in knowing that "the Lord *knoweth* all things from the beginning; wherefore, he prepareth a way to accomplish all his works among the children of men; for behold, he hath *all power* unto the fulfilling of all his words. And thus it is" (1 Nephi 9:6; emphasis added).

❧

Part of the mortal experience includes moments that are filled with discouragement and despair. During these times it may be hard to believe that God's will for us is good and that makes it especially hard to trust God's will. Turning to the Savior during these moments allows Him to shelter us from the full pain we might experience from these mortal trials. Through prayer and scripture study we can be reminded that He is in our midst and is our advocate with the Father.

I have learned that sometimes God's will is to send the miracle in a way we might not anticipate or expect. At first we may not see the abundance, but with time we will recognize the gift and realize that all along, and even through it all, His will for us was good. He knows exactly what we are in need of, even when we don't. And often it is only when we look back that we discover, hidden within the growing, the promise of enough, the abundance, the good that God will send.

Looking back over these moments will help us understand that abundance can be found in the form of tender mercies that show us the true nature of God. Line upon line these mercies are given as constant reminders of His hand in our life. President Henry B. Eyring taught as a member of the Quorum of the Twelve Apostles, "One of the ways God teaches us is with his blessings; and so, if we choose to exercise faith, the Holy Ghost will bring God's kindnesses to our remembrance."[3]

Keeping a journal of these tender mercies as they are given can help us see the Lord's hand in our life more clearly. And looking back, we can see that tender mercies in the form of blessings from God have been carefully placed throughout every moment of our lives, both the good times and the bad times, gentle reminders of God's love for us, a testimony of His will. Even more importantly, these tender mercies serve as a reminder that He is willing to send moments of abundance into our lives.

*Turning to the Savior during these moments allows Him to shelter us from the full pain we might experience from these mortal trials.*

I love the scripture that was given to the Saints at a time when they also struggled with a heavy burden. Although the burden was not taken from them, they were given a promise from the Lord that would sustain them through the trial. He promised, "I have much treasure in this city for you, . . . for there are more treasures than one for you in this city. . . . And I will order all things for your good, as fast as ye are able to receive them" (D&C 111:2, 10, 11).

It is a comfort to understand that Heavenly Father's will is to order *all* things for our good, as fast as we are able to receive them. Everything we experience in this life can be for our good. There is a silver lining, a blessing around the corner. Living the abundant life is learning to watch for the silver lining and trusting God's will enough to believe that even through the darkest of storms, the light will come.

I once participated in a youth activity that I will never forget. Jigsaw puzzles had been set out in small piles on several tables around the room. The youth were split up into different groups with about five kids in each group and assigned to complete a puzzle. There would be a contest to see which group could put together their puzzle first.

The teams went right to work, each trying to outdo the others as they attempted to finish the puzzle. As you can imagine it was quite loud, the room filled with the excited chatter of teamwork. An adult had been asked to stand behind every table to monitor the progress. Without drawing any attention to themselves, each adult had been asked to quietly whisper to the group in front of them, "I have the last piece of the puzzle in my pocket." Randomly, as the time went on, the adults would repeat the information, watching as the group frantically worked at the puzzle.

Minutes ticked on and not one group heeded the whispered words. Finally the groups were close to completion and it began to dawn on them that there was a problem—they were missing a piece of the puzzle. They crawled on the floor to look under the table, checked again inside the box, and asked each other if the missing piece could have dropped into somebody's pocket. And still, from the back of the group came the steady whisper, "I have the last piece of the puzzle in my pocket."

When searching produced no reward, the groups started yelling to the person in charge, "We're missing a puzzle piece." As soon as one or two groups had made the announcement, they realized that this complication must be part of the game. Frustrated they turned to the adult who stood behind them for advice and finally listened to the quiet whisper, "I have the last piece of the puzzle in my pocket." That was the key to understanding. The puzzle was completed, the game was over, and a lesson had been learned. There is One who knows the end from the beginning, whose will is for us to succeed, and who will send counsel and encouragement along the way.

How often do we find that our own life resembles this puzzle experience? We go along, putting together the puzzle of our life, trying to figure things out in our own way. When things don't go as planned we shuffle the pieces and try again—determined to find the solution by ourselves. Too often we struggle for too long on our own without success before we finally turn to Heavenly Father for advice. It is only after we humble ourselves enough to ask His will for us that we realize He holds the missing piece of the puzzle—a piece of knowledge that we may not have previously possessed. The answer may not be the one we were looking for, but we will feel that it is right. Daring to follow the counsel will lead us to discover the abundance He has in store for us.

The Lord stands beside us and patiently waits for us to turn our will over to Him, for us to ask and then listen for the quiet whisper of direction. He holds wonders in store for each one of us, and His counsel and direction will not be kept from us. When we learn to listen and follow His quiet promptings the puzzle pieces will begin to fall into place, and the abundance will come.

This then is the first principle for living the abundant life—learning to understand and trust God's will. With that increased understanding comes the ability to turn our own will over to the Father and allow Him to do wonders in our lives. Elder Neal A. Maxwell explained, "As you submit your wills to God, you are giving Him the *only* thing you *can* actually give Him that is really yours to give."[4] He said further, "It is only by yielding to God that we can begin to realize His will for us. And if we truly trust God, why not yield to His loving omniscience? After all, He knows us and our possibilities much better than do we."[5] The Lord is willing to do wonders in our lives, but we have to allow Him in. By submitting our will to Him we give Him full access into our life, allowing the wonders to begin, and the abundance to finally come.

God knows each of us individually. He loves us more than we can understand. It is just as true in our own lives as it was in the story of the loaves and the fishes, "He [knows] what he would do" (John 6:6). There is a miracle in store for every one of us. Elder Jeffrey R. Holland encouraged us to think about our future, our dreams, and our destiny. He said, "I believe that in our own individual ways, God takes us to the grove or the mountain or the temple and there shows us the wonder of what His plan is for us. . . . We see as much as we need to see in order to know the Lord's will for us and to know that He loves us beyond mortal comprehension."[6]

We must remember that God's will for us is good, that He knows the end from the beginning, and that He will order all things for our good. And at those times when we are uncertain about God's will for us, let us remember those moments when we have felt His love and His tender mercies, and consider that maybe right now His will is too good for us to know. As we turn our will over to Him, we will discover a life overflowing with the abundance of unexpected wonders, each testifying of the greatness of God.

*Abundance is*

TURNING OUR WILL OVER TO GOD
AND ALLOWING HIM TO DO WONDERS
IN OUR LIFE.

# Rondel

by George Macdonald

I do not know thy final will,
It is too good for me to know:
Thou willest that I mercy show,
That I take heed and do no ill,
That I the needy warm and fill,
Nor stones at any sinner throw;
But I know not thy final will—
It is too good for me to know.

I know thy love unspeakable—
For love's sake able to send woe!
To find thine own thou lost didst go,
And wouldst for men thy blood yet spill!—
How should I know thy final will,
Godwise too good for me to know!

# Make the Most of Today

Why does *believing* that God's will for you is
good allow you to *trust Him* more fully?

Have you ever taken the *time to ask* in
*humble prayer* what God's will is for you?

Do you believe *understanding* God's will
for you *will lead to abundance?*

The obvious solution was to dismiss the multitude and allow
them to return to the village to find food and shelter.

But this was not what He had asked of them.

And so they gathered to converse.

What did they have to offer?

# The Second Principle

*"And thou shalt rejoice in every good thing which the Lord thy God hath given unto thee."*

—Deuteronomy 26:11

There is a defining moment in the story of the loaves and fishes—it is the moment when the Savior asks the disciples what they have to offer to the multitude. They counsel among themselves to determine what they could, in a very real sense, bring to the table. In the end, what they had to offer was five loaves and two fishes, and from that small amount more than 5,000 people were fed. The same is true in our own lives. God will take whatever we have prepared, whatever we can offer, and increase it to create an abundance for us and others. It is our responsibility, just as it was for the disciples, to discover what God has blessed us with—to ask ourselves what it is that we have to offer.

It was the calling I always said I never wanted. And so, after the bishop extended the call, all I could do was cry. Twenty minutes later he prepared to leave our home and asked, "So, is that a yes?" I nodded a confirmation and he replied, "It's going to be fun. Wait and see, you're going to love it."

Completely overwhelmed, I walked into my bedroom and knelt down to pray.

Looking back now I would have to say the entire next week was one constant prayer. The prayer consisted of the same phrase repeated over and over, "Heavenly Father, what were you thinking? I am not capable of this. What is it you want me to do?" At the end of the week I planned a trip to the temple. After everything was settled at home I started the drive to the temple and I began the silent prayer again in my heart, "I am not capable of this responsibility. What is it you want me to do?" Immediately the Spirit whispered back to my heart, *"You took no thought save it was to ask."* My first thought was, "What does that have to do with anything?" I pushed the advice out of my head and focused on praying about the task at hand.

That morning the temple was busy. I love it when the temple is busy because it allows me some uninterrupted time to immerse myself in the scriptures while I am waiting. I picked up a triple combination and flipped it open. My temple scripture habit is to start reading wherever the scriptures open—it adds a little variety to my scripture study. On that day the scriptures opened up to Doctrine and Covenants, section 9. Imagine my amazement when I read the section and came to verse 7, "Behold, you have not understood; you have supposed that I would give it unto you, when you took no thought save it was to ask me." Obviously I had something to learn. In pondering what the message meant I realized that although I had asked for help in determining how to fulfill my new calling, I had never stopped to ponder what I might be able to bring to the calling. The Spirit had whispered the truth: I had taken no thought of what I had to offer, I simply asked Heavenly Father to tell me what to do.

I spent the next few days preparing to begin my new calling. My preparation included a personal inventory to see what I had to offer. For some reason, Heavenly Father had chosen me for this moment, this calling. Why? Was there someone I would be able to reach? Did I have a testimony of something I needed to share?

Each of us has a circle of influence. This circle extends beyond our church callings and into our everyday life, including our relationships with family and neighbors. We have been placed where we are for a purpose, even if it is to touch the life of just one person. I have come to realize that each of us is on an errand from the Lord; sometimes that errand has the title of a calling, most often it does not. Heavenly Father knows the power of our influence and He will place us where He needs us. It is up to us to determine what we have to offer in that situation, and, more importantly, whether we will offer our best. Relief Society General President Julie Beck counseled, "The Lord expects us to increase our offering."[7] I am confident that the increase of our offering will lead to more abundance in our life.

I love to watch movies that leave you with something to ponder at the end. Recently I had the opportunity to watch *Mr. Magorium's Wonder Emporium.* The heart of this story tells of a young woman who is desperate to recognize her full potential. Throughout the movie her mentor encourages her to become everything she is capable of, at one point exclaiming, "Your life is an occasion. Rise to it!" But still she struggles to define what that potential might be. During one tender scene she asks, "When you look at me, do you see a sparkle—something reflective of something bigger that is trying to get out?"

The movie reminds me of a general conference talk given by Elder Joseph B. Wirthlin in which he explains a divine truth, "There is a spark of greatness in every one of us—a gift from our loving and eternal Heavenly Father. What we do with that gift is up to us."[8] I believe that to be true. One of the most important opportunities we will have in this life is to learn to recognize what that spark of greatness is. Discovering what we have to offer is one of the keys to living the abundant life.

But sometimes that discovery process can be daunting. Often we find ourselves in situations that leave us feeling unfulfilled or inadequate. Sometimes we feel overwhelmed by a responsibility. Perhaps we think someone else can do a better job than we will ever be able to do. Other times we may feel like we are underutilized or overqualified for the situation we are in. We begin to compare ourselves to others. When feelings of inadequacy dominate our lives it can make it almost impossible to experience and recognize blessings of abundance.

We live in a society where our performance is judged by how we compare to others. This is not the Lord's way. He has given each of us our own unique set of qualities and talents, our own spark of greatness that will allow us to reach our full potential. At the end of our journey He will measure our level of success, but our performance will not be based on our success compared to how others did; He will judge us by looking at our hearts, "for the Lord seeth not as man seeth; for man looketh on the outward appearance, but the Lord looketh on the heart" (1 Samuel 16:7). Only He can fully understand how well we did with the gifts we were given under the circumstances that filled our lives. Abundance comes as we realize that we don't have to live up to anyone's expectations but His.

⁓✦⁓

My Grandma Belle often related to us the story of her life. She was born in 1907. Her parents were part of what she called "the high society" in Salt Lake City and were very wealthy. We used to love to hear her talk about her childhood, including how her mother went to San Francisco to have her evening gowns and fancy hats made. I loved to imagine the engraved calling cards her mother would carry in a silver monogrammed card case that named a certain afternoon each month when she would serve tea and ladies could come to call. I pictured the beautiful dining room where they ate, and a maid in a black dress with a white collar and cuffs who served all of their meals. My grandmother was her mother's only child, and Belle's life was filled with fancy dresses, exciting trips, and luxuries many would have never experienced in the early 1900s. It was a life none of us could imagine. By the world's standards she came from a situation of great abundance.

My Grandpa Mickey came from a family of sheepherders. He was a high school coach with a very meager income. On top of all that, he was a Mormon. My grandma's parents did not approve of him, and they made it clear that marrying him would mean that my grandma would have to leave behind all of the comforts she had grown up with. For the rest of her life, her parents never stepped foot into her home, only ever speaking to her on the front porch. They put all of Grandma's inheritance money in a trust that she had very limited access to until after my grandpa died. It seemed to us that she gave up everything of value in her life to marry Grandpa Mickey.

Grandma Belle never tired of explaining to us that her decision to marry my grandpa was the defining moment of her life. An account from her journal explains, "All that I have today, all that I am, the happiness and contentment of my life, has come about because I married a Mormon and joined The Church of Jesus Christ of Latter-day Saints."

*He has given each of us our own unique set of qualities and talents, our own spark of greatness that will allow us to reach our full potential.*

It was a great sacrifice for her to leave her family and the only life she had ever known, but it was one she never regretted. To the end of her life she believed the moments where she reached her highest potential did not have to do with the wealth she had come from, but the moments in her life when she was serving the Lord. President Thomas S. Monson spoke at my grandmother's funeral. In his remarks he said, "She was a

noble woman with confidence that came from giving herself to the Lord."

Whenever I find myself feeling inadequate or lacking confidence in what I have to offer, I try to remember that quote. Grandma Belle's story taught me that giving ourselves to the Lord may require a great sacrifice on our part. Often we will have to give up something to allow room for Him in our life, but it also taught me that a life directed by the Lord will lead to great confidence. Think of your own life. Is that spark of greatness missing? When you consider your potential in your profession, your family relationships, or your church service, are you satisfied with where you are?

Each of us will experience feelings of inadequacy. Rather than complain or wallow in self-doubt, we need to discover how we can regain that confidence by giving ourselves to the Lord. The Bible Dictionary explains, "The effects of true faith in Jesus Christ include an actual knowledge that the course of life one is pursuing is acceptable to the Lord."[9] We must turn our life over to the Lord. He alone knows what we are capable of. He alone knows the blessings that are in store for us. Therefore, His input becomes essential. Without it we will be incapable of reaching our full potential, unable to live the abundant life.

The story is told about the captain of a ship down in the South Atlantic. His ship had run out of fresh water, and the crew found themselves in desperate need of drinking water. Finally another ship passed by, and the captain signaled, "Send us water." Immediately the signal came back, "Let down your buckets, there is fresh water all around you. You are in the Amazon." Quickly the crew let down their buckets and realized it was true. They were floating in the stream of the mighty Amazon as it flowed out into the briny deep, and the water all around them was fresh.[10] There was an abundance of just what they needed—enough, and some to spare.

Have you ever felt that your bucket was empty? Moments when you are stretched to the limit so tightly that you wonder what you possibly have left to offer? On those days it seems especially hard to recognize our potential and we might find ourselves wondering if we even have any. I have learned that when I find myself feeling that way, there is only one solution—I have to refill my bucket. And just like the captain, I too have learned that there is living water all around me. I have found it in my scripture study, in reading the words of the prophets, and as I communicate with the Lord in prayer. Although there are many things that bring me pleasure and relaxation, nothing refills my bucket and helps me to recognize my potential as quickly as time spent with the Lord.

When we find ourselves trying to refill our own buckets in our search to determine what we have to offer, there are two priorities that should never be set aside. The first is to make scripture study a daily event. The second is to increase the frequency of our prayers. Our greatest desire should be to receive direction from the One who knows us best. When these two priorities become a consistent part of our life, we will find that we are building a relationship with the Lord that will allow Him to communicate with us on a regular basis. This will enable Him to give us needed course corrections and insights as we strive to keep our buckets filled during our quest to reach our highest potential. Giving ourselves to the Lord by utilizing the power of frequent prayer and consistent scripture study will lead us to discover the spark of greatness heaven sees in each of us.

If we prepare our heart before we read, we really can make our personal scripture study *personal*. Our preparation might include a simple prayer to ask for the Spirit to be with us as we read. This will allow the stories and verses we read to become personal to us, giving us personal answers, direction, and comfort. Our preparation might also include reading with a specific question or concern in mind. Answers will come as we study, filling our buckets and giving us needed direction as we try to determine what we have to offer. These answers will become plain and unmistakable as we learn to recognize how the Lord speaks to us through the scriptures.

Have you noticed that regular scripture study can offer valuable insights into the gifts we need, and can help us learn to see the possibilities of what our life can become? Some of the most wonderful attributes we can obtain come to us as spiritual gifts. These gifts are listed throughout the scriptures, but three places where we can begin to learn about them are in 1 Corinthians 12:4–11, Moroni 10:8–18, and Doctrine and Covenants 46:10–26. As we study daily and seek these gifts, our lives will become more abundant.

Our earnest and humble prayers can also open a direct line of communication with Heavenly Father. Several weeks ago my son, Caleb, and I were eating a snack after church. I asked what he had learned in his Young Men's class. He told me they had an amazing lesson on prayer. Then he asked a question, "Mom, why do we always have lessons telling us to pray so that we will receive answers, but they never teach us how to pray so that we will receive answers?" It was a question that set us on a journey of discovery.

The scriptures are literal when they encourage us to "pray oft unto the Lord" (1 Nephi 18:3), pray always (Ephesians 6:18), "pray without ceasing" (1 Thessalonians 5:17), "let your hearts be . . . drawn out in prayer unto him continually" (Alma 34:27), "give ourselves continually to prayer" (Acts 6:4), and to "pray every where" (1 Timothy 2:8). Why? Because praying constantly allows us to have an ongoing conversation with the Lord. When we pray frequently throughout the day and address specific needs, we open the door to receive more frequent and specific answers.

The Bible Dictionary explains, "Prayer is the act by which the will of the Father and the will of the child are brought into correspondence with each other. The object of prayer is not to change the will of God, but to secure for ourselves and for others the blessings *that God is already willing to grant, but that are made conditional on our asking for them.*"[11]

Frequent prayer gives us an opportunity to ask for blessings at all hours of the day—especially during those moments when we find ourselves running on empty. There are blessings that God is already willing to grant if we just take the time to ask. Elder David A. Bednar said, "Morning and evening prayers—and *all* of the prayers in between—are not unrelated, discreet events; rather, they are linked together each day and across days, weeks, months, and even years. This is in part how we fulfill the scriptural admonition to 'pray always.' Such meaningful prayers are instrumental in obtaining the highest blessings God holds in store for His faithful children."[12]

Caleb and I wondered how many blessings we miss out on daily because we don't remember to stop what we are doing and ask in prayer for them. We talked about how sometimes we felt we were not worthy to receive the Lord's blessings. Then we determined that when we choose to include the Lord in our lives by asking for His counsel and requesting what we need from Him on a continual basis, we will have learned how to pray so that we might receive more frequent answers. Alma encouraged, "Counsel with the Lord in all thy doings, and he will direct thee for good" (Alma 37:37). If you follow the footnote for the word "good," it directs you to the Topical Guide entry for "Abundant Life." Truly, if we counsel with the Lord in all we do, He will direct us to live an abundant life.

Turning to the Lord through consistent scripture study and frequent prayer will help ensure that our buckets are not only full, but overflowing. We too will find an abundance of just what we need—enough, and some to spare.

In the past few years the circumstances of my life have allowed me to increase my temple attendance. I like to go in the morning, and in those early dawn hours I feel as though the lights of the temple are welcoming me as I return. I have noticed a very significant blessing come into my life through this increased temple attendance—I find myself receiving inspiration from the Spirit more often during the course of each day.

It is one of the blessings promised to all those who attend the temple. The

Doctrine and Covenants says, "How beautiful upon the mountains are the feet of those that bring glad tidings of good things, and that say unto Zion: Behold, thy God reigneth! *As the dews of Carmel,* so shall the knowledge of God descend upon them!" (D&C 128:19; emphasis added). This scripture explains that those who bring a voice of gladness to Zion will receive a wonderful blessing—the knowledge of God will descend upon them "as the dews of Carmel." It is a beautiful promise, but it becomes even more significant when we understand what is meant by the "dews of Carmel."

Mount Carmel is a mountain range that can be found northwest of the Holy Land. In ancient times there was always a five- to six-month period with no rain. Without rain, the foliage growing on Mt. Carmel would normally wither and die. However, there is an unusual phenomenon that takes place on this mountain range. Great humidity produces moisture during this dry season, which results in 250 dew-nights on Mt. Carmel every year.[13] Because of this heavy dew, Mt. Carmel remains green all year long.

When I think of the image of dew descending, evenly and in abundance across the Carmel mountainside, I realize that God has given us a very significant promise. Herein lies the lesson of the "dews of Carmel": we are promised that knowledge will descend upon us in remarkable ways. If we are attending the temple regularly, then, even in times of drought, the knowledge we seek will come when we need it most. This abundance of knowledge includes the privilege of recognizing who we are and what we have to offer. Our frequent and consistent temple attendance will allow the Spirit to whisper to our heart the truth about our divine potential.

In my kitchen there is a sign that reads, "See the possibilities." It is there to remind me that each of us has a different potential, each of us has been given different gifts. It is important to recognize the good in others—but it is just as important to recognize the good in ourselves. President Spencer W. Kimball said, "The abundant life is . . . achieved as we magnify our view of life, expand our view of others, *and* our own possibilities. . . . The more we follow . . . the Master, the more enlarged our perspective becomes."[14] Learning to see the possibilities in ourselves and others allows God to create miracles from our offering—to fill our lives with abundance.

As we allow the Lord to play a greater role in every aspect of our life—including in our occupations, our relationships, and our service—miracles will happen and abundance will come. When we give ourselves to the Lord, our confidence will grow. It will require faith and effort on our part, and the knowledge we receive may require us to make changes in our direction, but through consistent prayer, scripture study, and temple attendance, the Lord will lead us to recognize that spark of greatness within us. We will discover the gift that He has blessed us with. What we do with that gift will enable us to live lives of abundance.

Imagine the possibilities!

What will you do with your gift?

*Abundance is*

RECOGNIZING OUR FULL POTENTIAL
AS WE GIVE OURSELVES TO THE LORD.

There is a spark of greatness within
    every one of us—a gift from our lov-
    ing and eternal Heavenly Father.
What we do with that gift is up to us.

Walk in joy.
Radiate happiness.
Be filled with wonder.

Fill your minds.
Reach out to others.
Create a masterpiece.
Walk with an inner fire.

Love the Lord.
Strengthen your testimonies.
Magnify your callings.
Enlist in great and noble causes.
Create sanctuaries of holiness and
    strength.

Live lives of abundance.

(Adapted from Joseph B. Wirthlin, "The Abundant Life,"
*Ensign*, May 2006, 99–102.)

# Make the Most of Today

How does it make you feel to *know* that Heavenly Father has given you specific *gifts* and that *within you* is a spark of *greatness*?

Take a *personal inventory*.
What *do you* have to *offer*?

Do you *believe* that *the Lord* can take what you have to offer and *make it more*?

What He asked would require sacrifice.

They would have to give of their own.

It was hardly enough for them, and the disciple could not help but ask,
What are they among so many?

# The Third Principle

## GIVE ALL YOU HAVE

*"The people of the church should impart of their substance, every one according to that which he had; if he have more abundantly he should impart more abundantly; and of him that had but little, but little should be required; and to him that had not should be given."*

—MOSIAH 18:27

I have always wondered about the small lad we read about in the miracle of the loaves and fishes. The scripture story does not give specific details and of all of the explanations I have studied about the part the lad played in the story, the account of Bible scholar Alfred Edersheim is my favorite. Edersheim explains, "There was a lad there who carried the scant, humble provisions of the party. . . . It was . . . evening when the disciples . . . asked the Lord to dismiss the people . . . but He would have them give the people to eat! . . . They were not to buy, but to give of their own store! How many loaves had they! . . . When Andrew went to see what store the fisher-lad carried for them, he brought back the tidings, 'He hath five barley loaves and two small fishes,' to which he added, half in disbelief, half in faith's rising expectancy of impossible possibility: 'But what are they among so many?'"[15]

From this explanation we are led to believe that what the Lord was asking from His disciples would require them to literally *give all* they had. This idea was not new to the men who followed the Lord; they were men who already knew the principle of giving all. They sacrificed their very lives to follow the Lord. It was from their willingness to sacrifice that the miracles came—the Lord took what they had to offer and made it more.

❦

"I have been waiting for your phone call."

Those were the first words out of the bishop's mouth after my dad introduced himself as the president of the mission where one of the bishop's ward members was currently serving. It had been a month since the elder had arrived in our mission. My dad could tell from the moment he saw the new missionary that he would be different from the rest. He was big and awkward and had some trouble mingling with the other missionaries. Several days after assigning him to his first companion, my dad received a distress call, "Help! My companion has already had two bike accidents. If we don't do something, he won't live until Saturday."

And so my dad had quickly put a phone call in to the young man's bishop. The bishop told my dad that he had spent sixteen months agonizing over whether or not he should send in this young man's mission papers. He explained that this elder came from the backwoods of West Virginia. No running water. No indoor plumbing. The boy's father was an alcoholic, and the family only attended church if someone picked them up. However, the boy really wanted to be a missionary. The bishop told my dad of the countless hours this elder had spent off by himself reading the scriptures. His scriptures were so worn out the bishop was worried to let him take them with him on his mission, but the bishop told my dad, "He loves those scriptures and he knows them." My dad reported the two bike accidents to the bishop, who replied, "It doesn't surprise me. He probably has never ridden a bike before."

I love to think of this elder's commitment to give all in his service to the Lord. Where other missionaries complained about having to be in a bike area without an air-conditioned car, this elder didn't say a word. When my dad assigned him to a bike area, he could have easily explained that he didn't know how to ride a bike, but he didn't. This elder had enough faith to realize that he was the Lord's missionary, and that Heavenly Father would help him accomplish anything his mission president asked him to do. He was willing to give everything to be a missionary even if it meant doing something he had never done before.

His story reminds me of the lyrics of a favorite missionary hymn, "I'll go where you want me to go, dear Lord. . . . I'll be what you want me to be."[16] In this case the lyrics could have ended with "I'll give what you want me to give." This elder knew that if he gave all he had, the Lord would take care of the rest. I often wonder if my testimony is such that I would be willing to sacrifice to help build up the kingdom of God as willingly as this elder did.

We do not have to be a missionary to give all we have. There are two significant ways we can give that will lead to an abundant life. One is by giving of our increase; the other is by giving of our time and efforts. Both require great sacrifice and faith, and both lead to abundance.

For many years our stake celebrated a Day of Abundance in September during the season of harvest. This day was devoted to helping those in our community who were in need. Members of our stake prepared for this event by gathering items to donate to local charities. On the scheduled evening we would gather together as a stake family. As people walked into the event, their arms were full to overflowing with canned food for the food bank, children's books for the literacy center, clothing for a children's shelter, and other items that could be donated to Deseret Industries. Dropping these items off to the designated locations, the families would then gather in the middle of a large field where the celebration was taking place. Here they could drop off homegrown vegetables at a farmer's market, help tie quilts, eat a small dinner, or watch a video presentation from the LDS Humanitarian Center.

*The Lord asks us to sacrifice through the payment of offerings and then, through that same sacrifice, He blesses us even more abundantly.*

The farmer's market was always a favorite stop during the evening. The area had six long tables where people could bring fruits and vegetables from their home garden. Every year the harvest was plentiful and every year the tables would be covered with fruits and vegetables. We would always wonder what we would do with all of it. But here was the magic—at the end of each table was a stack of brown paper sacks. Everyone who attended the event could come over to the farmer's market and fill a sack with produce to take home with them. Always, at the end of the evening, the bags had been filled and all the food was gone, each family taking some of the harvest home.

I would spend much of the evening walking from the designated drop off locations to the farmer's market and then through the quilt corner and across the small hills dotted with families eating together and celebrating the Day of Abundance. My eyes would fill with unshed tears as I was reminded of one of my favorite scriptures, "Your abundance may be a supply for their want" (2 Corinthians 8:14). I know that through the sacrifice of our stake, many lives were blessed abundantly.

Each of us can participate in our own Day of Abundance celebration once a month when we fast and pay our fast offerings. On this day our giving becomes a supply for another's want, and we have the opportunity as a ward to gather our efforts together to bless the lives of those among us who are struggling.

Great blessings are promised in Isaiah 58:6–11 to those who give of their increase by paying fast offerings. The promises are clear:

Your light will break forth as the morning.

Your health shall spring forth speedily.

Righteousness will go before you.

The Lord will be your rereward (or rearguard).

When you call, the Lord will answer.

The answers will be clear, turning darkness into noonday.

The Lord shall guide you continually.

He will satisfy your soul in drought.

You will be like a watered garden, like a spring of water, whose waters fail not.

Of all the blessings listed, my favorite is the promise that not only will our soul be satisfied in drought, but also that we will be like a spring of water, whose waters fail not. (When I read that poetic image, I can't help but be reminded of the wellspring of Cascade Springs I mentioned in the first chapter.) The scriptures truly teach us that the principle of paying fast offerings comes with a promise. If you take a moment to follow the footnotes under the word "spring" in Isaiah 58:11, you will find a reference to "Abundant Life" in the Topical Guide. What a wonderful connection: the promised spring represents our abundant life. It is interesting that the Lord asks us to sacrifice through the payment of offerings and then, through that same sacrifice, He blesses us even more abundantly.

When a gift requires sacrifice, what is given becomes more meaningful—both to the one who gives and to the one who receives. This principle is true of both paying fast offerings and obeying the law of tithing. Tithing is a principle with a promise—though the payment may require great sacrifice, we are promised great blessings in return.

President James E. Faust teaches us a great lesson on tithing with this simple example, "I was taught more about the spirit of tithing by President Henry D. Moyle, who lived in my ward when I was serving as a young bishop. One tithing settlement, President Moyle came in and declared, 'Bishop, this is a full tithe and a little bit more, because that's the way we have been blessed.'"[17]

The Lord has only asked that we pay ten percent as a tithe, but, like President Faust, I admire the generous spirit of President Moyle and his inspirational example as one who has learned to recognize the abundance that sacrifice brings.

Paying our tithes and fast offerings will help us to recognize the importance of sacrifice, of giving all, and will teach us an important principle of abundance— as we prove the Lord, He will be there to make up the difference. He has promised us, "the earth is full, and there is enough and to spare" (D&C 104:17).

Sometimes giving all we have requires us to give of our time. One of our family mottos is the "Be There" principle. This principle helps to govern how we give our time. The principle came into existence when my kids reached the age where they began to question if they really had to go to Stake Conference, or to that Young Men's activity, or to come home early from a weekend vacation to attend church on Sunday. (I hope I am not the only mother who has had to answer this line of questioning.) After quite a bit of thought my husband and I realized the answer was quite simple—and we instituted the "Be There" principle.

Each of us has the opportunity to raise our hand each time a new leader is called. That sustaining can include a Primary teacher, Young Men's leader, the Enrichment leader, the bishop, the stake president, even the prophet. Part of raising our hand to sustain that person means that we have committed to support that leader in his or her calling. And that support includes attending the lessons they teach, the activities they plan, or anything that requires our ongoing support. In our family the decision has been made quite simple—if a leader asks you to go, you will *be there*.

Jaroldeen Edwards, a dear friend of mine, once said, "The truth is, we do not know beforehand what the valuable part of an experience will be. It may not be the speaker, it may not be the activity, but it may be the making of a new friend, the encouragement of a leader, a word said to a downcast acquaintance, or just the opportunity to feel the satisfaction of having supported those to whom we owe our support."[18] When we are where we are supposed to be, giving all in our support, abundant moments will come.

My mother taught me that the "Be There" principle can encompass more than our church attendance—it can govern our lives.

The mother of the family I loved to babysit for in my youth was also one of my mom's best friends, Cindi. I can still remember running in from the carpool after school one day to tell my mom that Cindi had delivered her fifth baby and that he was stillborn. The news devastated our family and my mom felt an immediate prompting to go to the hospital. When she arrived the door was closed, but still the prompting remained, so she quietly entered the room. Hearing my mom walk in, Cindi turned to her and said, "I feel so empty." Unsure what to say or do, my mom hesitated for a moment. When no words came, she climbed into the hospital bed next to her dear friend and held her as they both cried. There was nothing my mom could do, nothing she could say, but she was there, in that moment, and that made all the difference.

A few days later Cindi's husband, Steve, told my mom how much it had meant to them that she had come. He had always assumed that when someone was in a trying situation it was best to leave them alone, to let them have their space. Steve told my mom he had learned a valuable lesson from her example. He explained that he would never again hesitate when one of his friends was in trouble, wondering what he should do or how he might help; the most important thing was just to be there.

Two weeks later my mom received a phone call from the fire department. My six-year-old brother had been hit by a school bus. Shaking, my mother tried to drive her car out of the driveway. Seeing her distress, her dear neighbor Cindi stopped her and drove her to the accident. When they arrived they could see ambulances, fire trucks, police cars, and the school bus. After making their way through a huge crowd they saw the medics loading my brother into the ambulance. His skull was fractured and his leg was injured. The medics told my mother she would have to calm down before they would let her get into the ambulance. Finally they set off for the hospital and our neighbors, worried about my mother arriving at the hospital alone, began trying to locate my father. Once the ambulance reached the hospital, nurses from the emergency room opened the ambulance doors to unload my brother. Just behind them stood our neighbor, Steve.

He didn't have to say a word; he was there.

President Spencer W. Kimball said, "God does notice us, and he watches over us. But it is usually through another person that he meets our needs. Therefore, it is vital that we serve each other. . . . The abundant life, of course, has little to do with the acquisition of material things. . . . The abundant life noted in the scriptures is the spiritual sum that is arrived at by the multiplying of our service to others."[19] Real service does not require a calling, it does not require money, it only requires a willing heart.

We live in a time of great affluence. Moroni cautioned us about the perils of living in this generation, "Why do ye adorn yourselves with that which hath no life, and yet suffer the hungry, and the needy, and the naked, and the sick and the afflicted to pass by you, and notice them not?" (Mormon 8:39). Living in these latter days comes with a great responsibility—we must remember to care for those among us, to sacrifice our wants to provide for the needs of another.

Mary Ellen Edmunds once said to me, "In times of adversity hopefully there will be a covenant person within reach." What is a covenant person? Elder D. Todd Christofferson explained, "We are part of a covenant people, a community of Saints who encourage, sustain, and minister to one another."[20] I believe that a covenant person is one who knows how to bear another's burden, to give comfort to those who stand in need, and who is willing to mourn until the joy returns.

I want to be someone like that.

We need to remember the difference between *giving* and *giving all.* The difference can be summed up in one word—sacrifice. It is through our giving that the Lord will bless us abundantly. Let us remember a line from a favorite hymn, which teaches, "Sacrifice brings forth the blessings from heaven."[21] When we give our all, through paying our tithes and offerings or through our service, we need not ever worry if it will be enough.

The Lord will make up the difference.

The scriptures remind us over and over again that through our giving the Lord will bless us abundantly. His promise is sure: "Give to every man that asketh of thee. . . . Lend, hoping for nothing again; and your reward shall be great. . . . Give, and it shall be given unto you; good measure, pressed down, and shaken together, and running over. . . . For with the same measure that ye mete withal it shall be measured to you again" (Luke 6:30, 35, 38).

*Abundance is*

**UNMEASURED BLESSINGS THAT COME AS A RESULT OF SACRIFICE AND SERVICE.**

# Give Ye to Me

by Hilary Weeks

The disciples watched the crowd
as they heard the Savior's words
And the afternoon sun began
    to fade
And seeing their need the Lord said,
    "Give them to eat,
Then we'll rest for a time by
    the shore."

"But Lord, there aren't enough
    fishes or bread
So how will the people be fed?"
And he said,

Give ye to me all that you have
    to offer
And I will bless it and I will make
    it more
And you will have all that you need
Though it seems there's not enough
I'll make the difference up
Give ye to me.

There are times in my life when I
    feel overwhelmed
And the days just slip through
    my hands
And even though I try, I fall
    further behind
And I wonder why I started at all
But somehow louder than the
    doubt and fear
There is hope in the words that
    I hear

Give ye to me all that you have
    to offer
And I will bless it and I will make
    it more
And you will have all that you
    need
Though it seems there's not
    enough
I'll make the difference up
Give ye to me.

# Make the Most of Today

*How* do you give?

What are you willing to *sacrifice*?

How would you *describe* the difference between
*giving* and *giving all*?

Think for a moment of one or two *individuals* whose
*sacrifice* or service has *influenced* your life *for good*.

How did you *know* they cared for you?

What did they sacrifice in their *giving*?

What can you *learn* about giving from their *example*?

The lad was in awe of these men he traveled with, for no matter what
the Giver asked, His disciples did not hesitate to obey.

Somehow these men had set aside their doubt, but he still could not help but wonder.

# The Fourth Principle

*"If they obey and serve him, they shall spend their days in prosperity,*
*and their years in pleasures."*

—Job 36:11

There is one proof at least of the implicit faith, or rather trust, of the disciples in their Master. They had given Him account of their own scanty provision, and yet, as He bade them make the people sit down to the meal, *they hesitated not to obey."*[22]

Much can be learned from this example. Even though every piece of knowledge the disciples possessed suggested otherwise, the Savior was planning to feed the multitude. It is interesting that the disciples did not question, nor did they doubt. Instead, they did not hesitate to obey. The disciples knew that their Master was a God of miracles. Their belief included faith in Him and trust in His power. Past experience had taught them what they must do. They prepared for the miracle by obeying the Master. Here, then, is another key for living the abundant life—our belief must be backed by obedience.

❦

How important is obedience to abundance? "There is a law, irrevocably decreed in heaven before the foundations of this world, upon which *all* blessings are predicated—And when we obtain any blessing from God, it is by *obedience* to that law upon which it is predicated" (D&C 130:20–21; emphasis added).

This scripture teaches us a significant principle. There is a law that governs the way blessings are given. God abides by this law, which was irrevocably decreed before the world began. This means, as much as He longs to bless us, He cannot, unless we are first obedient to the law upon which that blessing is predicated.

In the story of the loaves and the fishes, the disciples did not hesitate to obey the Savior's request, thus allowing the miracle to unfold. It is the same in our own lives. If we long for a certain blessing we must research and then obey the law upon which that blessing is bound, even if we don't understand it. Through our obedience, our testimony will grow and blessings will follow.

A blessing and its accompanying law can be found by studying the scriptures and the words of the prophets. Pause for a moment and think of three or four commandments. Those that come immediately to my mind are the law of tithing, the Word of Wisdom, and the covenants I have made. Each commandment contains a principle with a promise. Now, try to think of the blessing that is promised if we obey these commandments. The blessings that come from paying our tithing or keeping the Word of Wisdom are familiar because they are spoken of so frequently. However, we may not be as familiar with other laws and their predicated blessings.

Consider this. We are reminded once a week as we take the sacrament of the promise that "[we] may always have his Spirit to be with [us]" (D&C 20:77). But are the three commandments we promise to keep during the sacrament as familiar? (Willing to take on the Savior's name, to always remember Him, and to keep His commandments.) Sometimes the laws do not come as quickly to mind as the blessings do.

Here are a few other examples. In Mosiah 2:36 we read that if we are obedient to the commandment of always having the Spirit with us, we will be blessed, prospered, and preserved. In Doctrine and Covenants section 59 we are told that by being obedient to the commandment of keeping the Sabbath day holy we will not only be blessed temporally and spiritually, but in fact, we will live an abundant life. I have learned to watch carefully as I read my scriptures so that I can link each blessing or promise I come across with the law that governs it. Further research leads to greater understanding. We have been promised, "I, the Lord, am bound when ye do what I say; but when ye do not what I say, ye have no promise" (D&C 82:10).

It is our obedience that allows us access to these blessings. Obedience requires faith, trust, and belief. It is impossible to obey a Master we do not believe in. Our commitment and devotion to Him will determine the commitment and devotion with which we are willing to obey His commandments. Part of believing is doing our part. The Prophet Joseph Smith taught that faith is "the principle of action in all intelligent beings."[23] The Bible Dictionary explains that, "Grace cannot suffice without *total effort* on the part of the recipient."[24] As we listen to and obey the voice of the Lord, we have been promised that blessings will come.

*Through our obedience, our testimony will grow and blessings will follow.*

"And all these blessings shall *come on thee,* and *overtake thee,* if thou shalt hearken unto the voice of the Lord thy God. Blessed shalt thou be in the city, and blessed shalt thou be in the field. Blessed shall be the fruit of thy body, and the fruit of thy ground, and the fruit of thy cattle, the increase of thy kine, and the flocks of thy sheep. Blessed shall be thy basket and thy store. Blessed shalt thou be when thou comest in, and blessed shalt thou be when thou goest out" (Deuteronomy 28:2–6; emphasis added; see also Deuteronomy 28:8, 12).

Isn't that a wonderful promise? That *all these* blessings will not just come upon us, but in fact, *overtake us,* simply because we obeyed the voice of the Lord. Elder D. Todd Christofferson taught, "In times of distress, let your covenants be paramount and *let your obedience be exact.* Then you can ask in faith, nothing wavering, according to your need, and God will answer. He will sustain you as you work and watch. In His own time and way He will stretch forth His hand to you, saying, 'Here am I.'"[25] That is the promise of abundance.

❦

I love this quote: "Both abundance and lack [of abundance] exist simultaneously in our lives. . . . . It is always our conscious choice which secret garden we will tend."[26] I think of this secret garden when I remember the counsel the Savior gave to His disciples, "Consider the lilies of the field, how they grow" (Matthew 6:28). In the moments when I am in need of heaven's help as I search to discover abundance in my life, I find myself considering the lilies.

The Jerusalem lily is much more reminiscent of a poppy than the Easter lily we commonly think of. Those who have had an opportunity to raise poppies know that they come back year after year. But more important, they multiply abundantly, creating a beautiful landscape of color.

The Savior continued counseling His disciples, saying, "Wherefore, if God so clothe the grass of the field, . . . shall he not much more clothe you? . . . Therefore take no thought, saying, What shall we eat? or, What shall we drink? or, Where-withal shall we be clothed? . . . For your heavenly Father knoweth that ye have need of all these things" (Matthew 6:30–32). The Lord asks us to have complete faith in Him and in His ability to provide. And then He gives this important counsel, "Wherefore, *seek not the things of this world* but seek ye first to build up the kingdom of God, and to establish his righteousness; *and all these things shall be added unto you*" (JST Matthew 6:33; emphasis added). He asks us to trust and believe. The foot-notes from verse 33 tell us that our righteousness, or obedience, will lead to bless-ings *and* to an abundant life.

There have been many times in my life when I have found great comfort in this scripture. Often it has been at those times when I can't see any possible way that an abundance will come, and in those moments I remember what this scrip-ture encourages me to do: have faith and trust—the Lord will provide.

It is the law of the harvest. We are promised, "Whatsoever ye sow, that shall ye also reap; therefore, if ye sow good ye shall also reap good for your reward" (D&C 6:33). But we must also remember the end of that promise, found in John 16:33, "*In the world ye shall have tribulation:* but be of good cheer; I have overcome the world" (emphasis added). The law of the harvest requires us to be obedient and patient as we sow our seeds in the right time, place, and season, knowing that tribu-lation may come. The promised blessing of that law is that the Lord knows how long the growing season will be, and what the increase will bring.

Every year our family plants a garden. I will admit, we are not the most knowl-edgeable gardeners, but we do our best, and have tried our hand at onions, cu-cumbers, tomatoes, cantaloupe, peppers, and squash. One year the weather was especially hard to work with. It was too cold and there was too much wind. Every day I would check our garden and find that one or another of our plants hadn't made it through the night. So I made it a habit to stop at our local nursery to pick up a few more vegetable plants to replace the ones that hadn't survived. When I returned home I would carefully replant the small plants, some here, some there, wherever there was a lack. When the weather finally warmed, it seemed the only variety left at the nurseries came from the squash family, and as I planted I told myself that at least we would have a plentiful harvest of squash.

We worked in the garden all summer long—picking weeds, watering, and watching for the crops to appear. Those of you who are avid gardeners probably know what happened—when the harvest came it was not at all what we had expected! Long, skinny zucchini that were green on both ends, but brilliant orange in the middle, yellow squash with bright green zucchini caps, deep orange cucumbers, and butternut squash that were green and striped like cucumbers. It was a disaster! All of our hours spent to no avail—failure.

But as I have pondered that experience I have since changed my mind. There *was* an increase, just not the one we had expected. We experienced an increase of knowledge (I now know not to plant squash randomly and in close proximity again,) an increase of laughter as our family and friends waited to see what the harvest would produce, and an increase of support and unity as we found joy in the hours we spent together working in the garden rather than finding fulfillment in what came out of the garden. In the end there was certainly a bounteous increase, just not the one we had in mind. Sometimes our level of expectations for what we think we need can blind us from truly seeing the harvest Heavenly Father sends.

Paul says, "I have planted, Apollos watered; but God gave the increase. So then neither is he that planteth any thing, neither he that watereth; but God that giveth the increase. . . . And every man shall receive his own reward according to his own labour. For we are labourers together with God. . . . And ye are Christ's; and Christ is God's" (1 Corinthians 3:6–9, 23). I believe this to be true. We labor together with God, but it is He who gives the increase in every aspect of our life. We must have faith in Him, we must learn to trust that, when the growing season is over, the increase will come.

It is important to remember that the increase is not always found in temporal blessings or miraculous healings, sometimes the increase is found in spiritual growth. Each of our lives will include moments when we put all of our effort into a situation and when all is said and done, we feel that we have failed. I think of individuals or families who keep the commandments, pray fervently, study consistently, serve diligently, and still experience the challenges of mortality such as a wayward child, unfulfilled aspirations, remaining single or childless, or insurmountable health obstacles. I have learned that if we limit our vision to include only this mortal experience, we become shortsighted and fail to comprehend the full measure of the promised increase.

*We cannot underestimate the purpose of our mortal existence.*

We cannot underestimate the purpose of our mortal existence. We must not forget that life will include both the peaceful moments of Nauvoo and the painful moments of Liberty Jail. History shows that God's growing seasons include times when our faith is proven and found sufficient. Therein lies the increase. When we find ourselves in those Liberty Jail moments we must be willing to trust and labor together with God, reminding ourselves that Nauvoo's splendor lies ahead. Through our labor and obedience we can have faith that when the growing season is over, the increase will come.

Just like He watches the lilies of the field, God watches over each one of us, and He will provide for us. I love the promise the Lord gave to His apostles, if you "continue to preach . . . in all lowliness of heart, in meekness and humility, and long-suffering, I, the Lord, give unto [you] a promise that I will provide for [your family]; and an effectual door shall be opened for [you], from henceforth" (D&C 118:3).

The Lord takes care of His own.

When I was growing up there was one birthday tradition I could always count on. My grandma would make a special trip to the bank and withdraw money for a birthday gift. She made a point to ask for bills that were brand-new, crisp and clean. Then she would place the bills in a birthday card with written instructions that we were to use the money for something fun. One year I kept one of the dollar bills to use as a bookmark in my journal, as a reminder of my grandma's gift. I remember thinking to myself just before I got married that I would know we were never poor if I never had to use that one-dollar bill.

Early in our marriage my husband, Greg, had a severe illness that kept him out of work for several months. I remember sitting down to pay our bills at the beginning of the third month and after I had paid what we owed, we had $2.49 to last the rest of the month.

The thought crossed my mind that this might have to be the one-dollar-bill month—but I determined I would only use it if we were desperate. I considered the story of the lilies, and knowing that Greg and I were obedient in doing our very best to keep the commandments, I said a silent prayer in faith and then trusted that the Lord would help us figure out how to get by on $2.49 for a whole month.

Three days later, Greg's sister stopped by our apartment with a fifty-pound bag of potatoes that someone had accidentally left under a shopping cart at Albertson's. She figured that since we were newlyweds, we could probably use it. Little did she know.

A few days after that was Valentine's Day. I opened the mailbox to find a letter from my mom in California who had no idea how desperate things were. In the letter she had individually wrapped twenty one-dollar bills in Valentine's wrapping paper for Greg and me to use for something frivolous. (I never told her that our spending spree came from the grocery store.)

As unimaginable as it seems now, we got by that month with twenty one-dollar bills, a fifty-pound bag of potatoes, and $2.49. Just as the Lord took care of His lilies, He took care of our simple needs. You may not think we were blessed abundantly, but I believe we were—after all, we didn't have to use my grandma's one-dollar bill.

And as bad as things have sometimes gotten, we never have.

Elder Joseph B. Wirthlin said, "The abundant life does not come to us packaged and ready-made. It's not something we can order and expect to find delivered with the afternoon mail. It does not come without hardship or sorrow.

"It comes through faith, hope, and charity. And it comes to those who, in spite of hardship and sorrow, understand the words of one writer who said, 'In the depth of winter, I finally learned that within me there lay an invincible summer.'"[27]

In the midst of winter, our invincible summer will come from a deep and abiding belief in the One who helps the lilies grow; the One who promises to send blessings in our behalf. It comes from faith, trust, and obedience backed by belief. We find the abundant life in those moments when, with absolute faith and trust, we obey, and then believe, and then stand back as the miracle unfolds. God will provide the increase.

*Abundance is*

BLESSINGS PREDICATED ON
OBEDIENCE AND BELIEF.

# Consider the Lilies

by Roger Hoffman

Consider the lilies of the field,
How they grow, how they grow.
Consider the birds in the sky,
How they fly, how they fly.
He clothes the lilies of the field.
He feeds the birds in the sky.
And He will feed those who trust Him,
And guide them with His eye.

Consider the sweet, tender children
Who must suffer on this earth.
The pains of all of them He carried
From the day of His birth.
He clothes the lilies of the field.
He feeds the lambs in His fold.
And He will heal those who trust Him.
And make their hearts as gold.

# Make the Most of Today

Think of a *blessing* that *you* are in *need* of most.
What are the *principles* you would need to *obey*
in order to *receive* that blessing?

What specific *goals* can you set that will help you
to *increase* your *obedience* in that area?

The lad watched in amazement as the Giver took the
bread and gave thanks.

Such gratitude for this simplest of foods surprised the boy.

# The Fifth Principle

## REMEMBER GRATITUDE

*"They shall abundantly utter the memory of thy great goodness."*

—Psalm 145:7

One important principle we can learn from the story of the loaves and the fishes is that gratitude was shown before the increase. Remember, it was after Christ gave thanks for the simple provisions that the miracle came. There is great significance in this lesson—as we seek abundance, we must remember gratitude. Elder Joseph B. Wirthlin reminds us of the importance of being grateful for the simple things. He says, "Sometimes we should express our gratitude for the small and simple things like the scent of the rain, the taste of your favorite food, or the sound of a loved one's voice. . . . It changes our focus from our pains and our trials to the abundance of this beautiful world we live in."[28] Our ability to remember gratitude for even the smallest blessing has a direct influence on our ability to live the abundant life. Perhaps we could echo the prayer of George Herbert who said,

> *Thou that hast giv'n so much to me,*
> *Give one thing more, a grateful heart.*[29]

I do not think it is a coincidence that Thanksgiving comes before Christmas. I have learned that a season of gratitude always precedes a season of giving. Because of this, whenever I feel that I have nothing to give, I stop and allow myself a season of gratitude. Sometimes it is only after we ponder the simple blessings of our life that we realize that we do indeed have much to be thankful for. Often a miracle can be found waiting in the wings of the ordinary, everyday moments of our lives. When we recognize these small miracles, we learn to remember gratitude.

Recently I had the opportunity to learn a very important lesson about the need to set aside a moment to remember gratitude. Things were not going well for a young man in our neighborhood. He was faced with adversity, he was missing church frequently, he was making poor choices that required regular interaction with our local police department, and he was failing in school. Trying to remedy the situation, our bishop asked four families if they would be willing to help this young man. Each night, Monday through Thursday, this young man would go into one of these four homes for dinner and homework help.

The families who were asked to participate in these homework nights had the opportunity to participate in something miraculous—a tiny miracle hidden within the ordinary, everyday moments of their lives. Our family was one of those families. As I have seen how this experience has not only blessed the young man's life, but also ours, my heart is full of gratitude.

Our assigned homework night is Monday so this young man also stays for family home evening. Recently we had a family home evening lesson on gratitude. Each of our children has a family home evening journal and at the end of the evening we have journal time where we write down some of our thoughts on what we have discussed. We always start this journal time with a question and on this particular night we asked, "Write down someone who has made a difference in your life. What did they sacrifice to help you? What can you learn from their example of giving?"

Immediately everyone started writing, except for this young man. I leaned over to ask him if he needed help coming up with an idea and he said, "No, Sister Freeman, I know what I want to write about. I want to write about those four families whose homes I go into every week. I just don't have the words to say." I was reminded of one of my favorite scriptures in Alma where Ammon says, "I cannot say the smallest part which I feel" (Alma 26:16). The gratitude this young man felt for the love and service that had been shown to him was beyond words.

The change that took place in this young man's life over the course of a single year was amazing. Since the homework nights started, he has returned to church, there have been no phone calls to the police, and his last report card GPA was a 3.0. I believe it was the sincerity of his gratitude for the sacrifice of these families that allowed an abundance of miracles to come into his life.

*Often a miracle can be found waiting in the wings of the ordinary, everyday moments of our lives.*

One of my most prized possessions is a denim picnic blanket—a patchwork quilt with red bandana squares and denim pockets. The pockets are mine—they came from the jeans I wore all through my growing-up years. One of my favorite pockets on that quilt even has a zipper that still works. (My children like to save treasures from our outings in that secret pocket.) My Grandma Margie kept all of those pockets from the time when I was little until the time when I got married, and she sewed them up into the blanket that I love. I guess I should really call the picnic blanket the memory blanket. It is full of all of the wonderful memories of my childhood, but more important than that, it is full of memories of my grandma. The blanket has become a reminder of how grateful I am for her.

When I use the blanket I am reminded of lessons from Grandma Margie that I don't ever want to forget. My grandma was a giver and she taught me how to serve. She was one of those people who always knew just what to do. One of my favorite stories happened during one of the last winters of her life. Because the population of her ward consisted mostly of elderly people, the bishopric was handing out assignments for shoveling the walks in the ward, and one counselor commented, "We won't need to worry about Berkley Street; Margie will have already taken care of that." It didn't matter that she was sixty-eight years old, when she saw a need she took care of it immediately, she didn't wait for someone to ask.

My grandma also taught me to find happiness in the midst of adversity. I'll never forget moving to California the summer before my senior year. Grandma Margie came to help us pack up the house. She arrived every morning before I woke up and left after I was asleep. Moving is sad and at regular intervals during those final weeks one of us would break down in tears. Grandma was quick with a remedy. "One, two, three," she would say with enthusiasm, and the whole house would shout, "Hooray!" When we arrived at the Mission Home in Ventura,

Grandma did not come with us. But as we unpacked we found hundreds of yellow sticky notes scattered throughout the boxes. Written in Grandma Margie's happy handwriting were four simple words—"One, two, three—Hooray!"

We use the picnic blanket a lot. It has accompanied us to firework shows, picnics, lacrosse games, and late-night movies. Every time we use it I am reminded of my grandmother's life—a life lived abundantly, with fullness overflowing. She was a woman who had found the wellspring of abundance, and she taught me by example lessons to live by. The blanket is a visual reminder of the counsel that President Thomas S. Monson gave, "With gratitude in our hearts, may we fill our days—as much as we can—with those things which matter most."[30] Grandma Margie was a very creative seamstress, leaving behind more than the treasure that came from her sewing machine; somehow she wove lessons into my life, teaching me to fill each day with those things that matter most. I experience an abundance of gratitude for her every time I use that blanket. Within the gift itself she left me something to remember her by.

⚜

One of my favorite scripture stories talks about the importance of having gratitude reminders. The story of Hannah is found in the first book of Samuel. The scriptures tell us that when Hannah approached the Lord, it was out of an abundance of grief. Her overwhelming sadness is described as a "bitterness of soul" (1 Samuel 1:10). She wept sore, prayed, and did not eat as she prepared to petition the Lord. Finally, after all her preparation and years of waiting, Hannah pled to the Lord for the blessing of a child, promising that she would give that child to the Lord all the days of his life.

After Hannah petitioned the Lord, the scriptures tell us "the Lord remembered her" (1 Samuel 1:19). Every time I read this sentence my testimony of God's love is increased. I know that because He remembered Hannah in her abundance of grief, He will remember me in mine.

The story continues, "She bare a son, and called his name Samuel, saying, Because I have asked him of the Lord" (1 Samuel 1:20). Hannah was grateful to the Lord; in Samuel, she had found something to remember Him by.

*One way to remember what we are grateful for is to write it down.*

When Samuel was very young she took him to Eli, the prophet, and lent him to the Lord (1 Samuel 1:28). In so doing, Hannah was fulfilling the Nazarite vow she had made (1 Samuel 1:11), essentially consecrating Samuel unto the Lord, setting him apart for a special mission; a Nazarite vow could last a person's entire lifetime. "Lending" Samuel back to the Lord was the ultimate magnification of her gratitude for the gift. I can't imagine how hard it must have been to entrust the tiny child that she had longed for into the hands of someone else to be raised. But the story does not speak of sadness, instead Hannah bears testimony of the goodness of God saying, "There is none holy as the Lord: for there is none beside thee: neither is there any rock like our God" (1 Samuel 2:2).

Even though Samuel was not with her, Hannah remembered her precious gift from the Lord. In their time apart, she spent countless hours sewing for her son. And once every year she visited the beloved child that she had pled for and brought him what must have surely been a token of her love—a handmade little coat. The book of Samuel tells us, "Moreover his mother made him a little coat, and brought it to him from year to year" (1 Samuel 2:19). Just as I remember my Grandma Margie from the quilt she sewed for me, I am confident that Samuel wore each of those coats and thought of his mother, whose prayers had resulted in the miracle of his life. He must have known that in wearing those coats, he was wrapped up in her love—and the coats became something to remember her by.

Right away we know how important each of those little coats were to Samuel. If they hadn't been, they wouldn't have been included in the history of his life. When I read this part of the scriptures, it teaches me that one way to remember what we are grateful for is to write it down.

And Hannah was blessed with three more sons and two daughters.

And Samuel was not forgotten by the Lord.

In fact, Samuel became the prophet of Israel. When the Philistines came to battle against them, the people turned to him for advice and he told them, "Prepare your hearts unto the Lord, and serve him only: and he will deliver you. . . . Gather all Israel . . . and I will pray for you unto the Lord. And they gathered together . . . and fasted on that day" (1 Samuel 7:3, 5–6). But Israel was afraid. And they said to Samuel, "Cease not to cry unto the Lord our God for us, that he will save us. . . . And Samuel cried unto the Lord for Israel; and the Lord heard him" (1 Samuel 7:8–9). And Israel prevailed.

"Then Samuel took a stone . . . and called the name of it Eben-ezer, saying, Hitherto hath the Lord helped us" (1 Samuel 7:12). And Israel was grateful to the Lord. And the stone, Eben-ezer—the stone of help—became for Israel something to remember Him by.

Samuel taught the people of Israel a great lesson—the importance of finding a way to remember the things we are most grateful for. The stone became a reminder of their gratitude for what the Lord had done for them and of the abundant life that only His help can bring.

The story comes full circle. Hannah is grateful to the Lord for the delivery of her son. Samuel is grateful to his mother for the delivery of his homemade little coats. He teaches all of Israel to show gratitude to God by placing the stone of help,

Eben-ezer, where it would be a constant reminder of their delivery from the Philistine army. Samuel's story teaches us the importance of remembering gratitude and it is in remembering gratitude that we truly live the abundant life.

President Henry B. Eyring gives some needed counsel in this regard, "[I] urge you to find ways to recognize and remember God's kindness. It will build our testimonies." But then he gives us a caution, "It won't be easy to remember. . . . And the challenge to remember has always been the hardest for those who are blessed abundantly."[31]

He gives us two ways to learn to remember gratitude. Both are significant. He suggests, "You could begin a private prayer with thanks. You could start to count your blessings, and then pause for a moment. If you exercise faith, and with the gift of the Holy Ghost, you will find that memories of other blessings will flood into your mind. If you begin to express gratitude for each of them, your prayer may take a little longer than usual. Remembrance will come. And so will gratitude."[32] As a familiar hymn reminds us, it is only after counting our many blessings, and, in fact, naming them one by one, that we truly "see what God has done."[33]

The second suggestion closely relates to the story of Samuel. President Eyring says, "Tonight, and tomorrow night, you might pray and ponder, asking the questions: Did God send a message that was just for me? Did I see His hand in my life or the lives of my children? I will do that. And then I will find a way to preserve that memory for the day that I, and those that I love, will need to remember how much God loves us and how much we need Him."[34] Just like Samuel, President Eyring encourages us to find a way to preserve our memories of the times we have seen the Lord's hand in our life. Our remembering will lead to gratitude. Our gratitude will lead to great blessings. The blessings will lead to abundance.

"Verily, verily, I say unto you, ye are little children, and ye have not as yet understood how great blessings the Father hath in his own hands and prepared for you;

"And ye cannot bear all things now; nevertheless, be of good cheer, for I will lead you along. The kingdom is yours and the blessings thereof are yours, and the riches of eternity are yours.

"And he who receiveth *all things with thankfulness* shall be made glorious; and the things of this earth shall be added unto him, *even an hundred fold, yea, more*" (D&C 78:17–19; emphasis added).

*Abundance is*

KNOWING THAT WE CANNOT BEGIN TO UNDERSTAND
WHAT GREAT BLESSINGS THE FATHER HAS PREPARED FOR US,
AND LEARNING TO REMEMBER AND EXPRESS GRATITUDE
FOR THOSE BLESSINGS.

# COME, THOU FOUNT OF EVERY BLESSING

BY ROBERT ROBINSON

Come, thou Fount of every blessing,
Tune my heart to sing thy grace;
Streams of mercy, never ceasing,
Call for songs of loudest praise.
Teach me some melodious sonnet,
Sung by flaming tongues above;
Praise the mount; I'm fixed upon it:
Mount of thy redeeming love.

*. . . Here I raise my Ebenezer;*
*Here by thy great help I've come;*
And I hope, by thy good pleasure,
Safely to arrive at home . . .
Prone to wander, Lord, I feel it,
Prone to leave the God I love;
Here's my heart, O take and seal it,
Seal it for thy courts above.

(emphasis added)

# Make the Most of Today

⁓⊹⁓

Take a moment to *count your blessings*.
Make a *list*. Share it with those you *love*.

Can you *remember* a time when you saw the hand of *the*
*Lord* in your life? Did you remember to *write* it down?

*He began to hand the bread to His disciples and they, in turn, gave to the multitude, one by one, until each had received.*

*The people ate until they were filled, as much as they would.*

# The Sixth Principle

*"For I have learned, in whatsoever state I am, therewith to be content."*

—Philippians 4:11

Our God is a God of miracles. He delights in blessing us. This principle is shown clearly in the story of the loaves and the fishes. Elder James E. Talmage explains, "Taking the loaves and the fishes, Jesus looked toward heaven and pronounced a blessing upon the food; then, dividing the provisions, He gave to the apostles severally, and they in turn distributed to the multitude. The substance of both fish and bread increased under the Master's touch; and the multitude feasted there in the desert, until all were satisfied."[35]

As the miracle unfolded, the disciples did not just hand out one piece of bread and one piece of fish to each person. Instead, the people ate as much as they would, until they were filled—until they were content. That is the way the Lord gives. It did not matter to the multitude that "barley bread and fish constituted the usual food of the poorer classes of the region."[36] They were content with what they were given. It was "simple, yet nourishing, wholesome and satisfying."[37] Note the words *simple, wholesome,* and *satisfying.* In and of themselves, those three small details can help us learn volumes about learning to be content with what we have, to learn the meaning of simple abundance.

There used to be an ongoing argument between my two girls every night. They shared a bedroom and Megan, who was nine, liked to sleep with the hall light on, while Grace, who was six, liked to sleep with the door closed in complete darkness. Needless to say, bedtime always ended in an argument. So it was shocking one night to hear the girls get ready for bed and fall asleep without one word of contention.

After they had been asleep for almost an hour I decided to go up and investigate. The hall light spilled through the open door onto the double bed where the girls slept. I crept close to the bed to pull up the covers and noticed that something about Grace's face was not quite right. I couldn't tell exactly what was wrong, so I finally turned on the bedroom light. I looked down into Grace's peaceful face and burst out laughing.

I don't know if you are aware of this, but the Build-a-Bear company makes a very small, silky sleep mask with an elastic band just big enough to fit around a stuffed animal's head. Somehow Grace had managed to fit that sleep mask around her head and over her eyes. Obviously the lack of circulation to her head was not as important as falling asleep in the dark. With the mask on, Grace could go to sleep in complete darkness while Megan slept with the comfort of the hall light. Problem solved. Even though it was not ideal, both of the girls were content with the arrangement.

In Hebrews 13:5 the Lord tells us we need to learn to "be content with such things as ye have." This advice almost sounds foreign in the world we live in today. Everything about our society epitomizes the need for more. We want more toys, more room, more enjoyment. Being content with what we have requires us to step back from what the world teaches and reexamine our needs.

Sometimes, as in Grace's situation, we might have to be creative in learning to be content with what we have. Other times finding contentment may require choosing to look at our circumstances in an entirely different way.

Sometimes a life of discontent comes when we compare where we are in relation to those around us. Time spent wishing our life had gone a different direction can lead to dissatisfaction with the circumstances that are ours. Perhaps we echo the words of Alma, "I ought to be content with the things which the Lord hath allotted unto me" (Alma 29:3). But sometimes it is hard to know how.

I often reflect back to the year after my son Josh was diagnosed with diabetes. His diagnosis came on the heels of some other obstacles that in and of themselves were hard to surmount. At the culmination of that year I was emotionally exhausted and my life was filled with discontent. A large part of the problem was that I felt that somehow Josh's diagnosis had taken away my identity. I had become unexpectedly consumed with this new lifestyle I didn't want. The trademark of my life had always been my spontaneity. Now that was gone.

Someone once described what it felt like to be the mother of a child with diabetes. You go out and find the biggest rock you can carry and set it on one edge of your kitchen table. Now every single day, for the rest of your life, you will need to move that rock from one end of the table to the other end intermittently, ten times throughout the day. You can't forget—not even once. You must adjust your life to accommodate that arduous task. It is hard to be spontaneous when you are responsible for moving a rock.

I literally mourned the loss of our old life. I found myself obsessed with watching the lives of my neighbors and seeing how they seemed to be going just the way they planned. While we were struggling with major financial problems from unplanned medical bills, they were taking vacations to Disneyland. When school started, they talked about teachers who were cute, loving, and creative; I was desperate for a teacher who was organized and punctual enough to remind Josh to test his blood sugar and eat the snacks needed to keep his body regulated. They sent their boys off to Scout camp in joyful anticipation of a week of freedom; I was a nervous wreck the entire time.

It was really hard to talk myself out of wishing that I could live in their shoes rather than in mine, to learn to be content with the life I had been allotted. Finally one day I determined that Heavenly Father must have some advice to pull me through. I knew without a doubt that He knew what I was going through. I was certain that this trial was one that Josh and I had been prepared for before we came to Earth. So, I knelt down to pray and then pulled out my patriarchal blessing, hoping I would find some counsel there.

Isn't it interesting how you can read over a blessing hundreds of times, and still, just when you need it most, one line can take on a whole new meaning? That is what happened to me. On that day one line stood out to me: I was encouraged to have an optimistic approach to the life that was mine. I sat back and pondered the counsel. Part of the life that was mine was to be the mother of a diabetic child. Now, how was I supposed to do that optimistically?

It required a lot of prayerful thought. It also required creativity. I began by

*Unexpected blessings have given me the optimism, hope, and reassurance to face whatever the future holds.*

buying a brightly colored, fabric-lined basket to carry around the diabetes supplies we used throughout the day, instead of the small, medical, black pouch that came home from the hospital with us. Blessings have come in the form of medical staff that we have unexpectedly grown to love, medical advances that have unexpectedly made our life easier, and friends who have offered their continued support at un-expected and particularly trying times in our life. These unexpected blessings have given me the optimism, hope, and reassurance to face whatever the future holds. Finding creative ways to approach this trial optimistically has taught me to be con-tent with the life I was allotted. My contentment lies in the abundance of blessings I have seen along the way. Now when I look at our situation with an optimistic view, I realize that without embarking on this unexpected journey, we would have never recognized any of those unexpected blessings.

Our lives are very different from each other. The journey that my life will take and the journey that your life will take will be filled with different learning ex-periences unique to what we need. I often think of the journey the pioneers took. In the journal of one of my ancestors the entire journey is described with one simple sentence, "Left the Mississippi River and reached the Valley without seeing one particle of rain or snow." That sounds like the pioneer trek I want to take! Contrast that with the experience of the Martin and Willie Handcart Companies. How many of us would have been content to discover we would have to take that journey—one that included ice-filled rivers and handcarts stuck in eighteen inches of deep snow?

And yet, as certain as I am that I would not have chosen that journey, I am re-minded of the story of the man who sat at the back of a Sunday School class where there was sharp criticism given concerning that trek. That elderly man arose and said: "I ask you to stop this criticism. You are discussing a matter you know nothing about. Cold historic facts . . . give no proper interpretation of the questions involved. Mistake to send the Handcart Company out so late in the season? Yes. But I was in that company and my wife . . . too. We suffered beyond anything you can imagine and many died of exposure and starvation, but . . . *we became acquainted with [God] in our extremities.*

*If we choose to live a life where we recognize every good thing, we have chosen a life of abundance.*

"I have pulled my handcart when I was so weak and weary from illness and lack of food that I could hardly put one foot ahead of the other. I have looked ahead and seen a patch of sand or a hill slope and I have said, I can go that far and there I must give up, for I cannot pull the load through it. . . . I have gone on to that sand and when I reached it, the cart began pushing me. I have looked back many times to see who was pushing my cart, but my eyes saw no one. I knew then that the angels of God were there.

"Was I sorry that I chose to come by handcart? No. Neither then nor any minute of my life since. The price we paid to become acquainted with God was a privilege to pay, and I am thankful that I was privileged to come in the Martin Handcart Company."[38] This man learned what it meant to be content with the life he was allotted. It was as he embraced the struggle that he learned to appreciate the strength that comes from the Savior, and in doing so, he discovered what he was truly capable of. He found abundance in the journey.

Heavenly Father knows what we need—He also knows where we are needed. The different paths each of our lives takes reflects that truth. Often we may stop and find ourselves surrounded by people whose lives seem to be going perfectly. Perhaps it may appear that their journey contains fewer trials. We might find ourselves wondering how life's challenges were distributed, and questioning if life is fair. If we constantly find ourselves thinking *I wish my life had taken that route*, or, *That is the way my life was supposed to go*, we will never be content. When we become dissatisfied with our life, we risk missing the abundance of blessings our own journey will bring. We need to remember that no matter where our journey takes us, if our life is focused on Christ, we will not be disappointed. In the long run it won't matter if our journey takes us through eighteen inches of snow, or if we travel under the summer sun without one particle of rain, the only thing that truly matters is that our journey leads us to know the Lord, for "in Christ there should come every good thing" (Moroni 7:22). If we choose to live a life where we recognize every good thing, we have chosen a life of abundance.

It was an old tandem bike leaning against the garbage can waiting for pick-up. To Greg's utter embarrassment, I couldn't help but investigate. The handlebars were messed up, the brake line was tangled, the chains were broken, and the tires were hanging off the rims, but the structure of the bike was fine, and so I wheeled it home for a closer look. Moments later Greg and I stood shoulder to shoulder staring down at my new *treasure*. What Greg saw was a piece of junk, requiring hours of work. I pictured hours of fun and laughter as we learned how to ride together with one of our kids accompanying us in the baby seat that was perched on the back. Greg left, shaking his head. I called the Schwinn store and set up an appointment.

I will admit it was quite a struggle as Greg and I lifted the bike, which was too old to have been manufactured with light-weight titanium, into the back of the van. And I giggled as Greg backed out of the driveway with the "I can't believe you are making me take this piece-of-junk into society" look on his face. But it was an entirely different situation when he arrived home. "Come help me lift this bike out of the van," he said. "And don't scratch it! They've got it in perfect working order, and the shop guy offered me $1300 for it on the spot." Suddenly we owned an antique, but for me, the priceless treasure has been the hours of fun and laughter and the wonderful memories the old bike has provided.

Sometimes becoming content requires us to take what we have and make it more. This doesn't mean we have to settle, it means we find happiness in making the most of what we already have. Brigham Young counseled, "It is our duty to improve upon every blessing the Lord gives to us."[39] This advice can be true of every aspect of our life—our relationships, the home in which we live, even our occupation. Our perspective can be enlarged so that we can realistically look at where we are, and then set goals to improve upon that situation.

There is a wonderful lesson found in Psalm 118:24, "This is the day which the Lord hath made; we will rejoice and be glad in it." By our attitude and our willingness to adjust, we can take what we are given and rejoice and be glad in it. Often it will require quite a bit of effort on our part, but the end result will be worth it, and the combination of our efforts, combined with the pleasure that comes from achieving the goal, will lead us to contentment. That simple scripture can be used as a model for many different aspects of our life. For example, we could say, "This is the tandem bike which we discovered in the garbage; we will rejoice and be glad in it." The statement is true. With quite a bit of vision and hard work, we have found a treasure in that bike, one that we can rejoice and be glad in.

What if you were to apply that scriptural advice to your home? This is the home which we live in; we will rejoice and be glad in it. What is your vision for your home? Think about setting some goals and defining work projects that would make you more content with where you are. Our first thought often tends to lead us toward bigger and better—I want more room, new carpet, expensive décor. That might be the world's standard, but we can't always afford to keep up with the world, nor do we need to. You don't have to have a lot of money to improve upon your situation. I have found that even simple pleasures can lead to an abundance of rejoicing and gladness.

Contentment can be found by walking into a home that is freshly cleaned, because order always brings a certain amount of gladness. There is something about a spiced candle burning on the counter, fresh-cut sunflowers from the side of the road sitting in a vase on the counter, and chocolate-chip cookies in the cookie jar that all hint toward an abundance of contentment. It's a fresh coat of paint, a fire burning in the family room fireplace, ripe garden tomatoes growing in the backyard, or fresh bread cooking in the oven. All of these simple pleasures remind me of a home filled with rejoicing and gladness, a home in which we can be content. When we consider abundance I hope we will realize that it is not the size of our home that matters, it is the feeling within that home that becomes of utmost importance. Contentment comes from learning to rejoice and be glad, to make the most of what we have—in essence, to see the good things that already surround us.

*By our attitude and our willingness to adjust, we can take what we are given and rejoice and be glad in it.*

In the book of Alma we read about Amulek, a man of no small reputation, a wealthy man who lived a full life, surrounded by friends and family. He was obviously, by the world's standards, temporally blessed. He tells Alma, "Nevertheless, *after all this,* I never have known much of the ways of the Lord, and his mysteries and marvelous power. I said I never had known much of these things; but behold, I mistake, for *I have seen* much of his mysteries and his marvelous power; yea, even in the preservation of the lives of this people. Nevertheless, I did harden my heart, . . . therefore *I knew concerning these things, yet I would not know*" (Alma 10:5–6; emphasis added).

As blessed as he was, Amulek had not seen the good things. It was not until his heart was softened that he recognized blessings unmeasured. Then he was quick to acknowledge, "He hath blessed mine house, he hath blessed me, and my women, and my children, and my father and my kinsfolk; yea, even all my kindred hath he blessed, and the blessing of the Lord hath rested upon us according to the words which he spake" (Alma 10:11). When his heart was humble, Amulek could finally recognize the good things that were all around him.

Eight years after his conversion Amulek bore testimony again of the importance of being content with what we have. He encouraged, "I desire that ye should remember these things . . . that ye live in thanksgiving daily" (Alma 34:37–38). I believe that contentment and gratitude are closely related. I have found that when my life is filled with gratitude, I am far more content with my circumstances, because I am humble enough to see the good things.

I wonder how many of us are in the same place as Amulek was before his conversion. Do we see the good things in our life, or are we never satisfied, saying, "after all this . . . I would not know"? True contentment comes from learning to see the good things that already surround us, to become more mindful of the ordinary, and then to rejoice and find gladness in those things.

The Lord is mindful of each of us. He is aware of our needs and blesses us accordingly. Real contentment comes from our ability to recognize the hand of the Lord in our lives. When we soften our heart to see the good things, we will be reminded that the blessings of the Lord have indeed rested upon us, that He truly does send blessings upon our house.

We are encouraged to "Let your conversation be without covetousness; and be content with such things as ye have: for he hath said, I will never leave thee, nor forsake thee. So that we may boldly say, The Lord is my helper" (Hebrews 13:5–6). Although it goes against everything society epitomizes, we would be wise to set aside our desires for more and learn to become content with what we have. I love the counsel from Elder D. Todd Christofferson, "We might ask ourselves, living as many of us do in societies that worship possessions and pleasures, whether we are remaining aloof from covetousness and the lust to acquire more and more of this world's goods. . . . Perhaps we can learn to be content with what is sufficient for our needs."[40]

How much will the Lord bless us? If our hearts are soft and we understand what it means to be content and we learn to recognize the good things, He will bless us abundantly.

As much as we would, until we are filled.

*Abundance is*

FINDING CONTENTMENT BECAUSE
WE REMEMBER TO SEE THE GOOD THINGS.

# GRATITUDE

by Nicole Nordeman

Send some rain, would You send
    some rain?
'Cause the earth is dry and needs
    to drink again
And the sun is high and we are
    sinking in the shade
Would You send a cloud, thunder
    long and loud?
Let the sky grow black and send
    some mercy down
Surely You can see that we are
    thirsty and afraid
But maybe not, not today
Maybe You'll provide in other ways
And if that's the case . . .
We'll give thanks to You with
    gratitude
For lessons learned in how to thirst
    for You
How to bless the very sun that
    warms our face
If You never send us rain

Daily bread, give us daily bread
Bless our bodies, keep our children
    fed

Fill our cups, then fill them up
    again tonight
Wrap us up and warm us through
Tucked away beneath our sturdy
    roofs
Let us slumber safe from danger's
    view this time
Or maybe not, not today
Maybe You'll provide in other ways
And if that's the case . . .
We'll give thanks to You with
    gratitude
A lesson learned to hunger after
    You
That a starry sky offers a better
    view
If no roof is overhead
And if we never taste that bread

Oh, the differences that often are
    between
*Everything we want and what we re-*
    *ally need*

(emphasis added)

# MAKE THE MOST OF TODAY

*What are some specific ways you could learn to be more content with what you have?*

*Take a moment to recognize the good things in your life. What will you rejoice and be glad in today?*

*Even now, the miracle of it all, the gift, was beyond understanding.*

# The Seventh Principle

*"But behold, I, Nephi, will show unto you that the tender mercies of the
Lord are over all those whom he hath chosen."*

—1 Nephi 1:20

Elder James E. Talmage points out two important details about the miracle of
the loaves and fishes. First, the miracle came to satisfy "a present and pressing
need."[41] This was not a random miracle, it happened because a specific necessity
warranted it. Second, we realize that after the miracle occurred, something very
significant happened. Jesus asked the disciples to "'Gather up the fragments that
remain, that nothing be lost'; and twelve baskets were filled with the surplus."[42] As
the disciples walked through the multitude gathering all of the remaining food, we
come to understand that "an excess was supplied."[43] And, in fact, what remained
exceeded the whole of the original. This example increases our understanding of
the Savior's love—He is able to send miracles to satisfy present and pressing needs,
and what He gives will be enough, with some to spare.

There are only a few times I remember being allowed to stay up late when I
was little. One of those times was Easter, when *The Ten Commandments* (with
Charlton Heston and Yul Brynner) was shown on television. Every year I was

captivated as God led Moses to deliver the people of Israel out of the hands of Pharaoh. I saw the frogs, the blood on the doorposts, and the death of the pharaoh's son, and I knew that Moses' God was a God of miracles. Then I would lie in bed and wonder if God could still perform miracles like that today.

Moses told the people of Israel, "The Lord did not set his love upon you, nor choose you, because ye were more in number than any people; for ye were the fewest of all people: But because the Lord loved you, . . . hath the Lord brought you out with a mighty hand. . . . Know therefore that the Lord thy God, he is God. . . . And he will love thee, and bless thee, and multiply thee: . . . Thou shalt be blessed" (Deuteronomy 7:7–9, 13–14).

In the years that have followed since those long-ago Easter nights, I have learned that the Lord our God, He *is* God, and because He loves us, He will bless us in ways we cannot comprehend. In fact, He will orchestrate miracles we would never even think to ask for.

*He will orchestrate miracles we would never even think to ask for.*

This year the whole family went school shopping together. It was quite an experience. I felt pulled in every direction, trying to stop and focus on each of my four children individually while still observing the group as a whole. At one point in the excursion we stumbled upon a fantastic deal on shoes for Megan. The shoe boxes were stacked on top of each other in the middle of the floor, with no rhyme or reason for any of the stacks. We went through each of the boxes and found two pairs that might work. Megan absolutely loved one of the pairs that were sewn together with many different colors of brown leather, but they were half a size too big. The other pair was simple, just white leather, and they fit. She debated back and forth for some time and finally chose the pair that fit, because her sensible side tends to win over her frivolous side.

We spent several more hours shopping and then met up with my sister and her children who were also school shopping. We got into the cars to head out for lunch and Megan looked down and noticed that her cousin had bought the pair of multicolored brown leather shoes. Immediately, she broke down in tears. Because I had looked through every box of shoes, I knew there had been two pairs of those same shoes in the same size, so I asked Megan if she would like to trade. After a few minutes of explaining that it was okay if the shoes were a half-size too big because she would grow into them, Megan decided we should purchase the shoes she loved instead if the ones that were practical. So I took Megan's white leather shoes and the receipt back into the store to exchange.

Once inside I found the stack of shoes in even more disarray than before. I sat on the floor and began going through boxes. After looking through most of the boxes I began to panic—the shoes were not there. Quickly I said a small prayer, "Heavenly Father, please help me find those shoes. If they are anywhere in this stack, or even in this store, please open my eyes that I might be led to find them."

I continued to look. I finished the stack without success, so I started again. There were lots of people going through the stack, maybe I had missed them the first time, and besides, now I had Heaven's help. But I searched to no avail. The shoes were gone. It hurt my heart to think of going back to the car with the white leather shoes; I knew Megan would be so disappointed. As I turned to leave I repeated the prayer one more time in my heart, "If the shoes are somewhere in the store, let me be led to find them." Just then a young man came running to the back of the store, dropped a box of shoes on the pile, and then left. With hope in my heart I lifted the corner of the lid, and there were the brown leather shoes. I grabbed the box in both hands and ran to the register, a prayer of thanks in my heart.

When I got to the car I told Megan of my experience and said, "Every time you put these shoes on your feet you can remember that you have a Heavenly Father, who loves you." I explained to her that in the end it was not the type of shoes she wore that was important to Heavenly Father, *she* was important to Him, and because the shoes were important to her, they were important to Him.

It was a tender mercy in the middle of a shopping trip, an orchestrated miracle, and it helped us both to gain a small understanding of the love our Heavenly Father has for each of us, even in the tiny details of our life.

Several years ago my sister, LauraLee, asked for my advice with a problem. She had been suffering from some severe health issues that required her to get an MRI. Her symptoms were becoming progressively worse, and the doctor wanted the test done as soon as possible. The problem was that he had scheduled the MRI at the same time she was supposed to be taking a final in her statistics class at BYU. Because she was on scholarship with the BYU tennis team, her grades were extremely important. Her statistics teacher had made it clear at the beginning of the semester that her students absolutely could not miss the final exam. No exceptions would be made.

On Friday, when LauraLee found out when the MRI was to be scheduled, she e-mailed her professor to try to receive permission to reschedule the exam. By Saturday night she had not received a reply. My parents felt she should have the MRI even if it meant risking her statistics grade. But still my sister was desperate to make contact with her professor.

I suggested that we could write a second e-mail explaining the circumstance in more detail, knowing the teacher would receive it Monday morning and, we hoped, understand why she was not in attendance. "Is that all we can do?" LauraLee asked. "No," I remember telling her, "we can pray that somehow she will receive the communication and contact you." I told her that I knew that if it were really important for her to make contact with the professor, the Lord would hear our prayers and help us to find a way. "But how will we find her?" she asked. "I don't know," I remember saying. "Too bad she's not in my new ward, it would totally solve the problem." We all laughed and then I left for home.

I was speaking in sacrament meeting the next day, and I had invited LauraLee to come hear my talk. About halfway through the meeting a woman in the front of the chapel stood up to take one of her children out. When the meeting was over, LauraLee rushed up to me and said, "You're not going to believe this, but I think my statistics teacher is in your ward."

We went to investigate. Sure enough, the bishop directed us to the Primary room and the Primary chorister was, in fact, the statistics teacher. She laughed when we told her the story and told us, "The amazing thing is, I never have to take my kids out of church. I don't know what happened. What a coincidence." But we knew it was more than a coincidence. The Lord had heard our prayers and orchestrated a miracle. We were able to explain the situation and the professor not only allowed my sister to change the time of her test, but also sent a very kind e-mail to my sister saying, "Good luck on the final and your medical tests. I hope everything turns out to be okay. You are in my prayers."

Just like Moses explained to the people of Israel, our numbers do not have to be huge to warrant a miracle. Because He loves us, the Lord will bless us, one by one. And through those tender mercies we will realize that His love for us passes all our understanding.

*May we do as the disciples did and gather, or recognize, those tender mercies from the Lord that none be lost.*

It is important for us to remember that the Savior's love and His ability to perform miracles in our life won't prevent us from experiencing trials. LauraLee's story is a good example of this. On Sunday we experienced a tender mercy and witnessed the hand of the Lord in my sister's life, gaining an understanding that He was acutely aware of her circumstance. On Monday we learned that she did indeed have a neurological disorder that she would suffer from for years to come. The understanding that came from the miracle on Sunday was powerful. The trial that we faced on Monday was part of LauraLee's learning in this mortal experience, and would not be taken from her. But the Lord had made it very clear the day before the diagnosis that He was aware of her circumstance and was willing to send blessings along the way above all she could ask for or imagine. This tender mercy helped our family understand that His love would surround her and help her to endure.

A scripture found in Ephesians testifies of the reality of this love, "Christ may dwell in your hearts by faith; that ye, being rooted and grounded in love, may be able to comprehend with all saints what is the breadth, and length, and depth, and height; *and to know the love of Christ, which passeth knowledge,* that ye might be filled with all the fulness of God. Now unto him *that is able to do exceeding abundantly above all that we ask or think,* according to the power that worketh in us, unto him be glory" (Ephesians 3:17–21; emphasis added).

The Savior loves each of us. He will send blessings just when we need them most as a testimony of His love for us. Elder David A. Bednar taught us the importance of recognizing these tender moments in our lives, "A loving Savior [sent] me a most personal and timely message of comfort and reassurance. . . . Some may count this experience as simply a nice coincidence, but I testify that the tender mercies of the Lord are real and that they do not occur randomly or merely by coincidence. Often, the Lord's timing of His tender mercies helps us to both discern and acknowledge them."[44]

May we do as the disciples did and gather, or recognize, those tender mercies from the Lord that none be lost, and in so doing, we will come to know the exceeding abundance of the Savior's love.

*Abundance is*

UNDERSTANDING THAT THE SAVIOR LOVES US
AND IS AWARE OF OUR CIRCUMSTANCES,
AND THAT HE WILL SEND BLESSINGS
ABOVE ALL WE COULD EVER ASK FOR OR IMAGINE.

# IT PASSES ALL MY UNDERSTANDING

CHERI CALL

I told him, "You are a scholar;
You know things that I don't know
But I believe a God in heaven
Made everything below
And I know we are his children;
I've known it since I was two
But when it comes to being struck with awe,
I'm just like you
It passes all my understanding,
All the beauty we have here
From the majesty of the canyons
To a tiny baby's ear
And even when I can't believe it,
He still believes in me
It passes all my understanding"

# Make the Most of Today

⚜

Often what we might have thought of as an
*amazing coincidence* is really the Lord
orchestrating a *miracle* in our life.
Can you think of a time when you found that to be true?

*Look back* over the last several months of
your life. When was the *last* time you received a
*tender mercy* from the Lord?
What was it?

# Living the Abundant Life

*". . . having abundance of all things whatsoever they stood in need . . ."*

—Alma 1:29

There is one final element that is paramount to our search for abundance. Without it, we might live a productive life, but one greatly lacking in wonders and miracles. To discover this key let us review together all of the elements in the story of the loaves and the fishes. Gathered on that hill above Galilee were more than five thousand people, twelve disciples, five loaves of barley bread, two fishes, and one small lad. Everything that was required for the miracle was in place.

But the miracle would not have happened if the Savior had not come.

The same is true in our own lives. We may be able to set our course, determine what we have to offer, serve, remember gratitude, and find contentment, but without the hand of the Lord in our life the abundance will not come.

And so we learn this important truth from Elder Joseph B. Wirthlin: "The abundant life isn't something we arrive at. Rather, it is a magnificent journey that began long, long ages ago and will never, never end."[45] Abundance is not a destination, it is a journey. And it is a journey that is motivated by one clear and abiding principle—our testimony of the Savior. This testimony becomes not only the motivation for our journey, but the very foundation for an abundant life.

I cherish the moments that I have spent with my visiting teacher, Verda Dallon, who is ninety-eight years old. On one occasion my neighbor and I were sitting on Verda's front porch and she turned to us and said, "I want to tell you girls a story." I love it when she calls us "you girls," I feel like I am fourteen again. She began to relate to us a wonderful story of abundance.

Many years ago, in the late 1970s, shortly after her husband had retired, they took a camping trip together. Noticing a trailhead running alongside part of the river, Verda and her husband decided to attempt a short hike. They climbed up a hill next to the river and as Verda's husband admired the view, she went to work setting up a small monument of perhaps ten to twelve stones as a memory that they had been there.

Several years later they visited the campground again. As they had before, they took the short hike up the small hill and Verda found her monument and added a few more rocks. Then, some twenty years after that time, in the late 1990s, Verda visited the campground again. This time, when she took her short hike she made a startling discovery—her monument had grown. In the years since she had been there, others had built on her foundation, creating a large monument, an abundance, where her small pile of rocks had once stood.

The principle that I take from this story is this—without the foundation, the abundance would not have come. This same principle can be applied to our own life. If we can lay a foundation with "Jesus Christ himself being the chief corner stone" (Ephesians 2:20), and then add to this foundation throughout our journey, allowing others to do the same, I am confident that we will build something quite remarkable. That sure foundation will lead to an abundance. Our efforts along this journey will have a direct impact on the extent of our happiness. Leading an abundant life will allow us to find ourselves on the magnificent journey that Elder Joseph B. Wirthlin described, one that will allow us to live "after the manner of happiness" (2 Nephi 5:27), just like the people in 2 Nephi. I love Paul's definition for living this way; he counsels us to remember that, "Your rejoicing may be *more abundant* in Jesus Christ" (Philippians 1:26; emphasis added).

This then is the culminating principle—the abundant life must be founded upon a testimony of Jesus Christ. For it is only through Him that we will live a life of abundance, and in so doing, discover that abundance is part of every moment of our life, not the result of it. Remember how the Savior explained, "I am come that they might have life, and that they might have it more abundantly" (John 10:10). The reason that He came was so that we might have an abundant life. He is the wellspring that will bring the continuous source of supply.

Christ is the abundance.

And so we end where we began, with the discovery that if we long to live the abundant life, it is to One Source that we must turn. To the One who knows what He is about to do. The One who knows what we have to offer. Who encourages us to give all, to remember gratitude, to be content, to believe, and in so doing, to be led to understand His love. We must turn to Him, who is the wellspring.

Then we will recognize His hand in our life.

Then we will discover blessings unmeasured.

Then we will live lives of abundance.

For the Giver of Every Good Gift has promised us enough—and some to spare.

Abundance.

# The Seven Principles of Abundance

**Abundance is**
*Turning our will over to God and allowing Him to do wonders in our life.*

**Abundance is**
*Recognizing our full potential as we give ourselves to the Lord.*

**Abundance is**
*Unmeasured blessings that come as a result of sacrifice and service.*

**Abundance is**
*Blessings predicated on obedience and belief.*

**Abundance is**
*Knowing that we cannot begin to understand what great blessings the Father has prepared for us, and learning to remember and express gratitude for those blessings.*

**Abundance is**
*Finding contentment because we remember to see the good things.*

**Abundance is**
*Understanding that the Savior loves us and is aware of our circumstances, and that He will send blessings above all we could ever ask for or imagine.*

*Unto him that receiveth it shall be given more abundantly.*

—D&C 71:6

# Acknowledgments

I won't lie, this book has been a hard one to piece together because the topic is one I feel so passionate about. The revisions seemed endless, and I am sure I would still be tucked away writing if it hadn't been for those dear friends who have cheered this book into existence. Thanks to Kris Belcher, Shari Brandt, Julie Waller, Carolyn Apsley, Donna Lyman, Shane Walster, Hilary Weeks, Tasha and Rob Murphy, Shelly and Jeff Labrum, Victoria North, Angela Bennett, Tricia Remington, Josephine North, Mindy Pearson, Rena Doman, Rachelle Brooks, Jeff Jackson, Maryam Cheney, Mac and Leslie Oswald, Micki Neslen, and Pete and Robin Lund. Your willingness to add advice along the way has meant the world to me.

To my family, who loves me always, after all and anyways. I love you back.

To Simon, who knows exactly how to bring everything I write to life. I am a visual learner, and your illustrations allow the Spirit to touch my heart, prompting reflection and increasing my testimony.

A special note of heartfelt appreciation to Jana Erickson for taking the time to encourage, brainstorm, and breathe life into these seven principles.

A standing ovation to the team at Deseret Book—Lisa Mangum, Richard Erickson, Sheryl Smith, and Tonya Facemyer—who have perfected the art of taking a rough-hewn idea and creating a masterpiece.

And finally, to you, the reader, because even though every indication in our world suggests otherwise, some part of you believes in the promise of enough and the miracle of some to spare. This world needs more people like you.

# NOTES

1. Thomas S. Monson, "Finding Joy in the Journey," *Ensign,* November 2008, 85.

2. Joseph B. Wirthlin, "Come What May, and Love It," *Ensign,* November 2008, 28.

3. Henry B. Eyring, "Remembrance and Gratitude," *Ensign,* November 1989, 12.

4. Neal A. Maxwell, "Remember How Merciful the Lord Hath Been," *Ensign,* May 2004, 46; emphasis in original.

5. Neal A. Maxwell, "'Willing to Submit,'" *Ensign,* May 1985, 72.

6. Jeffrey R. Holland, "'Cast Not Away Therefore Your Confidence,'" *Ensign,* March 2000, 10–11.

7. Julie Beck, "Fulfilling the Purpose of Relief Society," *Ensign,* November 2008, 111.

8. Joseph B. Wirthlin, "The Abundant Life," *Ensign,* May 2006, 101.

9. LDS Bible Dictionary, s.v. "faith."

10. See Spencer W. Kimball, *The Miracle of Forgiveness* (Salt Lake City: Bookcraft, 1969), 147.

11. LDS Bible Dictionary, s.v. "prayer"; emphasis added.

12. David A. Bednar, "Pray Always," *Ensign,* November 2008, 42; emphasis added.

13. See D. Kelly Ogden, "The Testing Ground for the Covenant People," *Ensign,* September 1980, 55–58.

14. Spencer W. Kimball, "The Abundant Life," *Ensign,* July 1978, 4; emphasis in original.

15. Alfred Edersheim, *The Life and Times of Jesus the Messiah,* part 1, Reference Library Edition (Iowa Falls: World Bible Publishers, 1971), 681.

16. Mary Brown, "I'll Go Where You Want Me to Go," in *Hymns of The Church of Jesus Christ of Latter-day Saints* (Salt Lake City: The Church of Jesus Christ of Latter-day Saints, 1985), no. 270.

17. James E. Faust, "Opening the Windows of Heaven," *Ensign,* November 1998, 54.

18. Jaroldeen Edwards, *Celebration!* (Salt Lake City: Deseret Book, 1995), 104.

19. Kimball, "The Abundant Life," 4.

20. D. Todd Christofferson, "The Power of Covenants," *Ensign,* May 2009, 21.

21. W. W. Phelps, "Praise to the Man," in *Hymns,* no. 27.

22. Edersheim, *The Life and Times of Jesus the Messiah,* 683; emphasis added.

23. Joseph Smith, *Lectures on Faith* (Salt Lake City: Deseret Book, 1985), 1:9.

24. LDS Bible Dictionary, s.v. "grace"; emphasis added.

25. Christofferson, "The Power of Covenants," 22; emphasis added.

26. Sarah Ban Breathnach, in John Cook, comp., *The Book of Positive Quotations,* 2d

ed. (Minneapolis: Fairview Press, 2007), 342.

27. Wirthlin, "The Abundant Life," *Ensign,* 101–2.

28. Joseph B. Wirthlin, "Improving Our Prayers," *Ensign,* March 2004, 26.

29. George Herbert, "Gratefulness," in *The Complete English Poems,* ed. Josh Tobin (London: Penguin, 1991, 2004), 115.

30. Monson, "Finding Joy in the Journey," 87.

31. Henry B. Eyring, "O Remember, Remember," *Ensign,* November 2007, 67.

32. Eyring, "Remembrance and Gratitude," 13.

33. Johnson Oatman Jr., "Count Your Blessings," in *Hymns,* no. 241.

34. Eyring, "O Remember, Remember," 67.

35. James E. Talmage, *Jesus the Christ,* Classics in Mormon Literature (Salt Lake City: Deseret Book, 1982), 310.

36. Talmage, *Jesus the Christ,* 311.

37. Talmage, *Jesus the Christ,* 311.

38. As quoted in David O. McKay, "Pioneer Women," *The Relief Society Magazine,* January 1948, 8.

39. Brigham Young, in *Teaching of Presidents of the Church: Brigham Young* (Salt Lake City: The Church of Jesus Christ of Latter-day Saints, 1997), 179.

40. D. Todd Christofferson, "Come to Zion," *Ensign,* November 2008, 39.

41. Talmage, *Jesus the Christ,* 311.

42. Talmage, *Jesus the Christ,* 310–11.

43. Talmage, *Jesus the Christ,* 311.

44. David A. Bednar, "The Tender Mercies of the Lord," *Ensign,* May 2005, 99.

45. Wirthlin, "The Abundant Life," 102.

# INDEX